PRAISE FOR *RIGHT FROM WRONG*

"We are looking—now more than ever—for a moral compass that will help direct our children, a light to illuminate their path. In *Right from Wrong*, Mike Riera and Joe Di Prisco, tapping once again their gift for seeing the world through our children's eyes, provide both the compass and the light."

—Joan Ryan, columnist, *San Francisco Chronicle* and author, *Little Girls in Pretty Boxes*

"What matters most in the life of a child is the work that parents and other caring adults perform in the trenches of the day-to-day. Riera and Di Prisco mine those areas . . . while offering sound advice, great scenarios, real life dilemmas, terrific dialogue, and measured responses for what many parents already do with children."

—Brian Thomas, Assistant Upper School Head, The Catlin Gabel School, Portland, Oregon, and Founder, A Child's Book.com

"This book is a great gift to parents and teachers. As children journey toward developing an internal moral compass, wrong turns are inevitable. This book can help adults avoid harsh overreactions and transform these inevitable 'crises' into invaluable opportunities for teaching right from wrong."

—Sanford A. Newman, President, Fight Crime: Invest in Kids

"A wonderfully reflective parent's companion. . . . Through illustrative stories and ihsightful analysis, [the book] teaces us how to help our children be authentic, whole, and centered."

—Carlton H. Tucker, Head of Upper School, Princeton Day School, Pennington, New Jersey

"A modest gem of a book, *Right from Wrong* . . . shows us that growing up, for both children and parents, is a matter of losing and finding integrity, of falling out of and coming back to wholeness, again and again. What a great deal we have to learn from that lesson."

—Craig McGarvey, Program Director in Civic Culture at The James Irvine Foundation

"Integrity is central to virtually every decision your child will make . . . Di Prisco and Riera have a great deal of insight on this important topic and *Right from Wrong* offers great wisdom. It is a book every parent should read."

—Rick Clarke, Head of School, Redwood Day School,
Oakland, CA

". . . A profoundly important roadmap for raising a moral child in today's culture. Practical, specific, and poignant."

—Coreen Hester, Head of School, The Hamlin School,
San Francisco, California

"Like the parent and child development oracles they are, Riera and Di Prisco take us to the heart of the matter—how parents can help their children develop authentic, ennobling and durable core identities. It is hard to imagine a more essential or empowering message."

—Albert M. Adams, Ed. D., Headmaster, Lick-Wilmerding High School,
San Francisco, California

"In *Right From Wrong*, Riera and Di Prisco courageously address a topic central to the growth of healthy human beings. . . . Their counsel is balanced, relevant, compelling and wise."

—Tony Paulus, Head of School, Green Hills School,
Ann Arbor, Michigan

"Finally, a parenting resource that puts integrity . . . where it belongs: front and center to everything we do. This is a wonderful guide for parents as they accompany their young children on their on-going journeys to being true to themselves."

—Bodie Brizendine, Head of School, Marin Academy,
San Rafael, California

RIGHT
from
WRONG

RIGHT
from
WRONG

....

Instilling a Sense
of Integrity in Your Child

MICHAEL RIERA, PH.D.
JOSEPH DI PRISCO, PH.D.

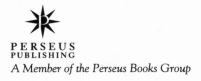

PERSEUS
PUBLISHING
A Member of the Perseus Books Group

Copyright © 2002 by Michael Riera and Joseph Di Prisco

All rights reserved. No part of this publication may be reproduced, stored in a retrieval system, or transmitted, in any form or by any means, electronic, mechanical, photocopying, recording, or otherwise, without the prior written permission of the publisher. Printed in the United States of America.

Library of Congress Control Number: 2003101192
ISBN 0-7382-0802-7

Perseus Publishing is a member of the Perseus Books Group.
Find us on the World Wide Web at http://www.perseuspublishing.com.
Perseus Publishing books are available at special discounts for bulk purchases in the United States by corporations, institutions, and other organizations. For more information, please contact the Special Markets Department at the Perseus Books Group, 11 Cambridge Center, Cambridge, MA 02142, or call (800)255-1514 or (617)252-5298, or e-mail j.mccrary@perseusbooks.com.

Text design by *Brent Wilcox*
Set in 11.5-point Goudy by Perseus Publishing Services

First paperback printing, April 2003

1 2 3 4 5 6 7 8 9 10—04 03

*Dedicated to the memory
of my father-in-law, William Moore Twadell.*
—MR

*Dedicated to my godchildren,
Isabel, Joe, Lucia, and Sam.*
—JDP

Here are your waters and your watering place.
Drink and be whole again beyond confusion.

—**Robert Frost, "Directive"**

CONTENTS

ACKNOWLEDGMENTS

We thank our colleagues, friends, associates, and family members who contributed, whether they knew it or not, to this book. We also want to thank our teachers, including those who taught us in school, who embodied integrity in their professional and personal lives. In particular, we thank:

Elizabeth Trupin-Pulli, our literary agent, a friend, and a writer's best ally.

Marnie Cochran, our editor at Perseus Publishing, asker of the best questions. Also, Lolly Axley, Leigh Weiner, and Marietta Urban of Perseus.

Especially, all those we buttonholed and asked to speak with us about integrity: Rick Clarke, John A. Gray, Robert J. Kelly, Carolyn Libby, Lori Mazon, Elise Miller, Kim Smith, Cynthia Traina, Peter Twadell, Susie Twadell, Lindy West, Valerie Wright, Dean Young, and Shafia Zaloom. We are sure we have left out many people to thank because while we worked on this book, no one was safe.

All our students and their families at all the schools where we have worked.

Finally, and most important, our families:

Megan Twadell-Riera and Lucia Riera.

Patricia James and Mario Di Prisco.

Introduction

Integrity Is the Compass Within

Why should we be in such desperate haste to succeed, and in such desperate enterprises? If a man does not keep pace with his companions, perhaps it is because he hears a different drummer.

—Henry David Thoreau, *Walden*

It is in youth that we plant our chief habits and prejudices. . . . In youth therefore the turn is given; in youth the education even of the next generation is given; in youth the private and public character is determined.

—From a letter written by Benjamin Vaughan,
in *The Autobiography of Benjamin Franklin*

Very high on any wise list of dreams for our children is the hope that they do indeed become people of integrity. Of course, we may also hope that they enjoy success and health and status and happiness, but we know that if they are lacking in integrity, all that will prove hollow. We also realize that if they have integrity, they will be, despite any setback and discouragement, people whom we will admire as well as people who are proud of themselves. After all, their integrity is one thing—perhaps the only thing—that can never be taken away by anybody else. It is the unfailing compass within that always gives them a true reading north, that tells them how far away they may be from home and how to return home. It is the source of their identity.

Integrity is as difficult to define as, say, identity or love, and for the same reasons. As we intend the term, integrity is nothing less than authenticity, an internal sense of rightness and wholeness. As such, honesty, for instance, is an indispensable starting point, as is the effort to represent oneself accurately, fairly, and reasonably, at home, at school, in relationships with family and others. At the same time, integrity implies respecting others and oneself.

In other words, integrity is a notion that cuts across psychological, moral, developmental, and social categories. And as much as we parents wish to guarantee results, we know integrity is not the product of reading to our children from a prepared script. It is subtler than that. And although integrity is essential for living well, there is no equivalent of a defibrillator we can implant in our children's chests to jump-start their moral lives.

Stephen L. Carter, author of *Integrity*, defines the concept this way:

> The word *integrity* comes from the same Latin root as *integer* and historically has been understood to carry much the same sense, the sense of *wholeness*: a person of integrity, like a whole number, is a whole person, a person somehow undivided. The word conveys not so much a single-mindedness as a completeness; not the frenzy of a fanatic who wants to remake all the world in a single mold but the serenity of a person who is confident in the knowledge that he or she is living rightly. The person of integrity need not be a Gandhi but also cannot be a person who blows up buildings to make a point. A person of integrity lurks somewhere inside each of us: a person we feel we can trust to do right, to play by the rules, to keep commitments. Perhaps it is because we all sense the capacity for integrity within ourselves that we are able to notice and admire it even in people with whom, on many issues, we sharply disagree. (italics in original)[1]

Perhaps, then, integrity is not *something* to be achieved. In this sense, it is more like bravery, loyalty, kindness, and all the other virtues. We can never quite have it, and the instant we think we possess it, it slips away. It may not be a thing at all, or if it is, we can only know its outlines, and even then only partially and incompletely. Tim O'Brien, our greatest writer about Vietnam, defines *courage* in terms that would be useful to apply to integrity:

> Sometimes the bravest thing on earth was to sit through the night and feel the cold in your bones. Courage was not always a matter of yes or no. Sometimes it came in degrees, like the cold; sometimes you were very brave up to a point and then beyond that point you were not so brave. In certain situations you could do incredible things, you could advance toward enemy fire, but in other situations, which were not nearly so bad, you had trouble keeping your eyes open.[2]

Sometimes we hear people speak of someone *having* integrity. And we all think we know what that means. But for us, to *be* in integrity implies a struggle—an ongoing and continual commitment to be true to oneself and to be fair to one another—as well as a search.

Integrity is the compass within each of us. It points us in the direction we need to travel. Without a compass like that, our lives become nothing more than a succession of events and experiences. If we do not know where we are going, we are lost. With a compass, our lives become journeys. And only with integrity do our journeys achieve meaning. As such, there is nothing more important to the project of parenting children than promoting integrity, and it is something that we must work on from the earliest years.

Integrity, essential as it is, is untreated by most parenting writers. Search the indexes of their books and you will not often find references to integrity; certainly, you will never find it to the same extent that you find mention of, say, self-esteem or character building or morality. This is curious, and we think all parents upon reflection may feel the same way. After all, true self-esteem and character and morality are predicated upon integrity.

We have a theory as to why it is so difficult to write about. Achieving integrity is a distant goal for all us, one we will never perfectly achieve. In that goal, we, as the authors, are one with everyone we admire and one with you, the reader. It is certainly why the subject has challenged us so personally, so profoundly. To be sure, neither of us claims to be a paragon of integrity, and that admission serves both to embolden and humble us.

Integrity is only fully appreciated under complicated circumstances, often under duress, often in disappointment and loss. The sad truth is that often one learns to value integrity most just after compromising it. That is, even though integrity is an absolute value, one comes to appreciate integrity through the messy, relativistic, day-to-day struggles of growing up. No wonder parenting writers flinch. They have two choices: Ignore it, or write a whole book on the topic.

We may be foolhardy, but we take Door Number Two.

Right from Wrong makes the promotion of integrity in our children possible, feasible, and creative. Their integrity is not simply something that happens as a result of family stability, unconditional love, healthy genes, or good luck; it happens because we make it important. Growing up is full of moments of joy and pain, but if our children do not develop integrity, they will be unable to understand, affirm, or prize them.

Right from Wrong is a book about how we as parents shape the growth of our five- to twelve-year-old children and, specifically, about how we find and form integrity in them. There are many books devoted to children's growth—emotional, psychological, moral, and social. And while this book addresses topics pertaining to the everyday lives of families with school-age children (bullying, sibling rivalry, family crises, puberty, the Internet, school yard violence, homework, family dinners, the media, honesty, and so on), it does so, we hope, with a difference. We intend to make explicit the connection between growth and the formation of integrity. We view parents and children through that crystalline lens because we think that is the most natural, pragmatic, coherent, yet visionary way for parents to develop healthy child-rearing practices.

In one respect, this book evolved from our earlier book, *Field Guide to the American Teenager*. In that book we show how teenagers grow up out of the purview of their parents. Parents are crucial in the lives of their adolescents, but the terms of their engagement in their kids' lives have dramatically changed. This is the time when parents must go beyond the hopes of managing their teenagers' lives and instead need to learn how to exercise influence. From our point of view, and based upon our experience and research, parents who exert the most positive influence upon their teenagers are those who have been concentrating throughout the childhood years on integrity.

As a practical matter, therefore, we write *Right from Wrong* with one eye looking toward what the parents of children can do now to raise healthy school-age children and another on the groundwork for healthy adolescence. We do this because it is adolescence, more than any other phase of life, that sends shivers down a parent's spine. Ask parents of teenagers about their children's younger years and they all say it feels as if it happened a minute ago and they long nostalgically for the days gone by. (It is one of the curiosities about most books on adolescence that that same wistful tone appears again and again—everybody wishes for a past that cannot be recaptured, when we were the centers of our children's universe.) Kids grow up fast, and parents need to stay in the moment with their school-age children even while at the same instant they prepare them for high school and adulthood.

In *Right from Wrong*, we show how, from very early on, children are tuned in to integrity. They yearn for wholeness within themselves and within their families. It is never easy or simple to promote integrity, and being honest often exacts a high price. The only consolation for parents and children alike is that there is no reasonable alternative. If we do not have integrity and do not value integrity in ourselves and in our children, we have very little on which to base a healthy relationship.

Examining parenting through the lens of integrity sheds new, and sometimes counterintuitive, light on traditional parenting assumptions. For instance, you will see how a misunderstanding of the role of praise in your child's development can lead to the undesired outcome of entitlement. Or when you administer disciplinary consequences, you can, instead of merely exercising power, use your authority and presence to help your child come to value the integrity he or she compromised. What's more, you will also come to realize the almost spiritual connection between integrity and intuition. In the end you will come to sense that as you assist your children to tune in to integrity in their lives, you will be able to worry about them less and appreciate them more. That is, the focus on integrity allows for less anxiety over rules and consequences and more room for spontaneous joy and love in your family.

Covering a wide range of topics—an after-school fight, a blowup on a soccer field, the death of a beloved family pet, the diagnosis of cancer in a parent, the discovery of porn sites on a child's computer, a shoplifting incident—this book introduces parents to the nuances and developmental realities of their child. We see how we can foster integrity in mundane and even surprising contexts, for instance, in how we respond to that archetypal childhood question "Is there a Santa Claus?" Every single day your child undergoes a potentially formative experience. Integrity factors in the way your child plays on the playground, or gets dressed for school, or treats a younger sibling. But it is formative only because you *form* the connection between your child's experience and his or her integrity.

Integrity begets integrity—and in very down-to-earth ways. Sane, creative, and compassionate parenting is consistently rooted in the practice of integrity. As parents, we know we are in integrity when:

- We stand our ground but are ready when the ground shifts underneath the feet of our children (starting school, puberty, graduation, experimentation). That means we ask questions and listen carefully to the answers as well as the silences; that also means we freely admit our mistakes and make generous allowance for kids' being kids. (See, for instance, chapters entitled "The Reality of Santa Claus," "Taking What Isn't Yours," and "Honesty.")

- We commit ourselves wholeheartedly to the process (discipline, education, relationship) while at the same time emphasizing absolutely the health and safety of our children. Kids need limits. They thrive within boundaries, and they need protection from making poor choices. They are children. ("The Shock of Emerging Sexuality," "Loss," and "Illness in the Family")

- We stay strong before the spectacle of imperfection but never let ourselves or our children give in to discouragement. ("Sportsmanship" and "Tattletales, Truth Tellers, and Name-Callers")

- We remember not to take personally any instances of failure or letdown, but we also make sure to give credit to our children when they do the right thing for the right reason. ("The Shadow of the Internet," "Cheating," and "The Fight")

Families are joined by love and compassion and commitment to each other, but it is the shared stories that define and characterize their lives together. Stories are the heart and soul of all families, and this book is about those moments. In *Right from Wrong*, we employ the same structure of *Field Guide to the American Teenager*. *Right from Wrong* combines stories of children in their natural settings with compassionate, in-depth analysis and pragmatic counsel. We show children negotiating the dramas of daily life, mostly at home and occasionally at school, on a field, in a store. Each chapter features two or three elements: a narrative, perhaps one or more conversations, and a section called "Notes Home." At the heart of each is a representative tale, based upon real-life incidents and experiences of children searching for meaning in their lives.

As psychologists, novelists, and memoirists have taught us, young children are explorers and philosophers. They struggle from early on in their lives to come to terms with the deepest questions of life and death, love and family, self and other. Each story in *Right from Wrong* presents a freeze-frame instant of a child and a parent reaching out for clarification, insight, support, and relationship—and therefore, integrity.

* * *

At the beginning of Maurice Sendak's classic *Where the Wild Things Are*, Max is wearing his wolf suit and making mischief, and as a result, he is disciplined: sent to bed without eating. Feeling powerful, he ventures off to the magical world where the wild things are and where he is summarily anointed their king. "Let the wild rumpus start!" he encourages the creatures of his imagination, and sure enough, it does. Eventually, he comes back home; however, it is the home that exists in his mind and heart, the place he can never finally leave even when he tries. And that's where his dinner and his family are still waiting for him.

Our children are imperfect, just like us. The world is full of very wild things. No wonder we parents worry and fret and question ourselves. All this to say that our soundest hope is to keep the dinner hot and to stay involved during those inevitable moments when our children seem to be beyond our control, at the mercy of forces we can sometimes only barely remember or understand. When our children are whole, when they feel authentic to themselves, when they grasp beyond words how important their own integrity is, however, we can nurse a beautiful hope based upon the most pragmatic insight into their dreams and struggles. Like Max, our children ultimately, and with lots of help from us, find their own way. Like Max, sometimes our children will disappoint us and themselves. Also like Max, though, they are always and already heading home, back to us and back to themselves.

Let the wild rumpus start.

Taking What Isn't Yours

How Do We Use Discipline to Foster Integrity?

[O]ne's origins are not romantic. Like the act of birth, they're merely the seeds of the life we're given—messy, tumultuous, mundane.

—**Maria Laurino, *Were You Always an Italian?***

A POCKETFUL OF TROUBLE

–One–

Tricia was frustrated *and* proud. Since giving birth to Sam five years ago, she had almost grown used to such emotional balancing acts. *Almost.* She had studied a little psychology in college, but only after becoming a parent did she experience how conflicting emotions could reside next to each other in her heart. Sometimes this recognition did not leave her feeling strange or unsettled in the least bit. *Sometimes.*

"Sam! It's time to go home. You can play with your friends again tomorrow."

Sam yelled back at her: "Mom! Just a little longer!" Then, to accentuate his demand, he put his head down and pedaled his friend's bike faster as he circled the kindergarten playground for what must have been the tenth time. And that was ten times within the two minutes Tricia had been waiting at the curbside.

Yes, she was frustrated to have him ignore her and her patient (until a second ago) requests. Only twelve school days had elapsed since he'd begun kindergarten.

Now that she recalled it, the very first day, and, really, those first two weeks, had been marked by another magnitude of frustration for her. The first moment Sam realized he was going to be left at school was even more traumatic than the time he had leaped off the pediatrician's table after catching a glimmer of the booster shot needle. As for that first day, Sam had been silent the entire ride, but as soon as Tricia turned off the engine, he turned the volume way up.

He begged not to be left at school, then he whined, then he yelled, and then he sobbed. By the time they by some miracle reached the doorway of the classroom, Sam was clutching Tricia's neck and had his legs wrapped around her waist. He was incapable of articulating a word. He could only wail and shake and squirm. Fortunately, Sam's teacher, Ms. Roberts, was good-natured and, after twenty years of teaching, experienced with these kinds of scenes. Had Tricia been able to look around at the other parents, she would have known that she and Sam weren't unique; plenty of other families were experiencing comparable opening-day ballistic drop-offs. But what parent could remain calm in this type of situation? Especially Tricia, a single parent who, whenever something went amiss, lapsed into the fallback default feelings of doubt and guilt and inadequacy.

But Sam and Tricia together had moved through that adjustment to kindergarten. Sure, Tricia was late for work during those first weeks, but fortunately, her boss understood; in a rare moment of personal revelation, she told Tricia that she and her husband had had the same problem with every single one of their three children. She had even offered some useful advice, which Tricia remembered for a day but had since forgotten.

After a few days of hanging around at the back of the classroom—with one other parent—Tricia began to sense that Sam was finally feeling at home. Slowly she cut back on her time in the room. And just last week the whole drop-off and good-bye ritual was reduced to an efficient ninety-second ritual of putting the lunch away, quick hugs and kisses, and a brisk "Have a fun day."

"You, too, Mommy," he replied, nearly bringing her to tears—of relief.

Only now, as she watched Sam circle the playground yet again, she wondered if perhaps they had been too successful: Now she couldn't get him to *leave* school.

"*Samuel. Nathan. Cochran!*" Word by emphatic word, syllable by slow syllable: the universal cry of parents on the brink of meltdown, which kids across the world know all too well. So did Sam.

"See ya tomorrow, Ricki. My mom says I gotta go now." Sam scooped up his *Whoosh Whoosh* lunch box and reached out with his free hand to his mom. She took it warmly. She was putty in his five-year-old hands.

—Two—

"So, how was school?"

"You know Hector? He had a bloody nose."

"Is he OK?" Tricia asked in a hushed, horrified voice.

"Yeah. You put your head down when you get a bloody nose, not back."

"But he was OK, right?"

"He gets bloody noses sometimes—it's OK, teacher said. Louisa went on a airplane with her grandma and grandpa to Sam Diego. Where's Sam Diego?"

Tricia told him *San* Diego was far away.

"Louisa's grandpa is a policeman, but he doesn't shoot bad guys."

"Is Louisa your friend?"

"She's a *girl*."

"I guessed that."

"Mom, can I watch *Whoosh Whoosh* when we get home?"

Of course, why should today be any different from every other day? While she wasn't proud of her daily thirty minutes of parenting by TV, even if it was PBS's *Whoosh Whoosh*, which was a pretty good show, actually, she couldn't imagine it any other way, either. He needed the time and routine to decompress from his day at school, and she needed the time to catch up on the household chores. Skipping that show wasn't an option in either of their minds. Still, they both must have enjoyed the ritual of Sam's asking each day on the ride home because that's the way it always played out.

"Sure you can. But remember, no crying when the show is over and I ask you to turn off the television."

He was amenable.

Even though the thirty minutes of television was lately stretching into more like forty-five or fifty minutes, Tricia always held the line about the TV going off at her request. So far, Sam was fine with that.

"But first we need to stop at the store for a few minutes. I need to pick up some groceries." The grocery was her local store, and when she could, she preferred shopping there to the chains.

"Why?"

"You want dinner tonight, don't you? That's why."

"I don't want to go to the store. I want to go home and watch TV."

"And you can, right after we go to the store."

"Mom! That's not fair. I want to watch TV now and I want to go home now."

"I want to go home, too, but we don't always get what we want when we want it." Did she just say that? She sounded just like her mother. "Sam, I know you want to watch television. And I know you don't want to go grocery shopping with me, but I need you to be a big boy and help me with the shopping." Appealing to his sense of responsibility usually got her, at the very least, his begrudging cooperation. "And, if you're real good, maybe we can get you a special treat."

"Really?"

"But only if you're good."

"What kind of treat? A chocolate bar?"

Where did that come from? Sam had certainly watched his fair
share of television, and not all of it PBS, but so far their house had
been a candy-free zone. Tricia was, she would perhaps concede, extreme in her insistence upon nutritious food, but still, a candy bar?
She wondered where he was learning this stuff. The unofficial
kindergarten curriculum probably included more than reading,
writing, and arithmetic.

"We'll find something special—but no candy, it's too close to
dinner." She knew the logic didn't hold. Why would a candy bar
ruin his appetite more than a banana? But she held her breath and
hoped. And then she quickly added: "Besides, you know how I feel
about candy."

"But I *want* a chocolate bar."

"How about we get some popcorn instead? We'll make a bowl for
you and a bowl for me, right after dinner." There, she thought, two
birds with one stone: a swift end to the candy-bar discussion and a
guarantee of a healthy appetite for dinner.

"My own bowl?"

—Three—

Tricia was feeling pleased with herself as she rounded the corner
into the den/television/play/living room. After all, they had been
home for only thirty-five minutes and she had already stowed the
groceries, boiled the water for tonight's pasta, reheated the sauce
she had made over the weekend, and even prepared Sam's lunch
for the next day. Not bad, she thought.

"Sam, time to turn off the television. Then please wash your hands and help me set the table."

"Just a little bit longer, Mom. *Please.*"

"Sam. Remember what you agreed to? The television goes off when I ask."

Sam rolled off the sofa, walked to the set, and turned it off. And that's when she saw it, on the sofa—the unmistakable black-and-white wrapper of a chocolate bar crumpled up around the silver foil.

For Tricia, it was a moment of cognitive dissonance she remembered learning about in her college psych course. Her jaw dropped while her brain came to a complete stop. Sam was surprised and a bit concerned to see his mom like this, until, that is, he realized her eyes were trained on the candy-bar wrapper. He sat back down.

Then, for the second time in one day, this mom uttered her son's complete name. *"Samuel. Nathan. Cochran."*

There was no place for Sam to hide, and he stood up once more. "What?"

"Where did that candy wrapper come from? And what happened to the chocolate bar inside it?"

That was when Tricia had her second moment of cognitive dissonance. As Sam began to mutter a reply, she was close enough to see chocolate traces at the corner of his mouth and to detect the aroma. "Sam! Where did you get that candy bar?"

"I don't know. I just had it."

"Sam, sit back down. We need to talk."

He and his mom both took their seats on opposite ends of the couch. His eyes looked straight ahead, away from hers.

"Sam. I need you to tell me the truth. Where did you get that candy bar? Someone at school?"

"No. Nobody at school."

Then, for the third time in what seemed as many minutes, Tricia entertained two incompatible thoughts at the same time. Sam is an honest child and—"Sam, did you take that from the store?"

His sad bearing said it all, and the enormous teardrops slipping down his cheeks confirmed what Tricia already knew: Samuel Nathan Cochran had stolen a candy bar.

NOTES HOME

Many families may well find an account of a kindergarten child stealing a little bit familiar and more than slightly disquieting. The authors themselves know this sort of thing both from firsthand experience with their own children and from accounts narrated by other parents. Most children, and certainly almost all five-year-olds, who take a candy bar from a store are not destined for a life of crime. In the remarks that follow, we are going to shine the light on the somewhat hidden corners of Sam's experience and sketch the bigger picture of this child's stealing—which is much more charged than a search for the instant gratification of a chocolate bar. As we follow the trail of motivation, so to speak, we will illuminate the ways in which integrity figures into this scenario, including some perhaps not completely expected ways. We begin, therefore, with a consideration of the most pressing issue of a five-year-old's life: the transition that consists of starting school.

First Day(s) of School

Who among us can forget our introduction to school? Strange kids everywhere. The unknown teacher. A foreign room. Abandonment. Fear. Astonishment. Milk and cookies. Structured playtime. New friends. Scissors and paper and hamsters and kickballs. Your own hook for your coat. Your own special toy or blanket or book that you cling to.

Even though many children attend preschool, kindergarten is still a great divider in our lives, when we take the first steps out of the absolutely secure world that is home into the new world fraught with mystery. As a marker in our development, it rivals, on one end, learning to crawl and, on the other, learning to drive a car. The whole world opens up before our eyes, and we are in it in a new way.

The first days of every school year (even through high school) have a lot in common with the first days of kindergarten. As a parent, therefore, expect the vulnerabilities and regressions and the acting out—which begin to take place even before the time school begins. The transition from summer to school is enormous for every child and, therefore, for every family. So do not get thrown off when you witness bouts of crying, or flare-ups of anger, or sudden onsets of coughing, or a return to a timidity that you believed had been outgrown. On the other hand, do not underestimate what is going on, either. Remember that what they are experiencing feels very real, and what they need from you is an acknowledgment of their turmoil, your presence, and your reassurance that they will be fine when they go to school the next day. The transition, to kindergarten in particular, lasts longer than one day; it will take weeks, and even longer, for your children to become acclimated to this new environment.

Transitions

Sam steals during a period of transition. He has just left school (just been dragged away, effectively) and is on the way back home. His new friends and his new teacher and his new kindergarten life are now all being replaced by his mom and the structures of domestic, family life. If it sounds simple, it really is not. He is changing gears (all right, grinding them as he downshifts), gradually reorienting himself in a far different realm from the one through which he has been traveling all day. In psychic and emotional terms, it can be hard, even wrenching, work—decompressing, mulling over his experiences, falling back into the terrain of home.

Sometimes we parents can forget how taxing this can be. But as adults, we surely know otherwise. We learn soon enough that the commute home can prove beneficial to our marriages and other relationships. If we turned around from our jobs at five o'clock and instantly confronted our friends and our mates, the first things out of our mouths might be complaints and self-justifications and expressions of disappointment—all carryovers from the day and matters normally best left unsaid. (And by the way, that's why when our kids become fifteen or sixteen, they will sequester themselves in their rooms, not to seal you off but to contain themselves, to listen to music, to talk on the phone, to answer their e-mails, and, in general, to figure out what just happened at school all day—which is why they can barely hear your question, "How was school today?")

Transitions, then, are those in-between times—just after ending one activity and just before beginning another. Of course, everyone every day goes through a variety of transitions. Children do, too: from sleep to waking up; from home to school; from class to the playground; from the playground to class; from school to home; from sunshine to twilight; from being awake to being asleep. The betweenness of such transitions makes each a potential moment of vulnerability and regression, and there is no predicting which. That is, four days in a row bedtime is smooth as can be, but on the fifth night, your son falls apart. Or suddenly, after school, your daughter is at a loss as to how to go to her friend's house next door to see if she can come out and play. The unexpected occurs routinely during transitions. And each time, the reason behind the outbreak is a fresh mystery, encouraging us all to yearn for the inspired patience and the analytical gifts of Sherlock Holmes.

Sometimes the behaviors that offend us correlate with conflicts that are left unresolved—on the other side of that transition. Your daughter is angry with her teacher, so she starts a fight with you; or your son is annoyed about being teased at lunch, so he takes it out on his younger brother by antagonizing him. Popular psychology labels these behaviors "acting out," because in these instances, your kids act out before your very eyes their frustration; it is called acting out because you become the audience for the performance, which is hardly ever consciously rehearsed.

Sometimes these offending actions (or nonactions, or words) are inspired by anxiety over the future—a new baby-sitter, a house being remodeled—in which case consistent routines are usually adequate to reduce anxiety and eliminate most negative behaviors. Picking up our children at the same time each day and employing the same patterns of conversation—*How was school today? Who did you play with? Tell me about something that was fun today. Tell me about something that was difficult today*—helps ease them away from their school day and prepare for their after-school day. Coming home to another set of routines (a snack, feeding the cat, changing clothes, whatever) helps them settle into their after-school routine.

Sometimes hurtful behaviors are imitations, or replays, of other people or friends they have just left behind. Hearing the older kids tell a dirty joke or using a vulgar word may lead them to try out the same behavior on you during the ride home. In these cases, simple limit setting and redirection works best. *We don't talk that way in our family. Let's talk about something else. Who did you eat lunch with today?*

Still, at other times they act out because they are bored. Remember, they are coming away from something—school, in this case—that was stimulating, and they are now refocusing on new kinds of stimuli or on creating new stimuli for themselves. A regular routine is usually enough to discourage this type of acting out.

When your children act out, whatever the reason, you hope to discern just what experience or difficulty they are enacting. It can be a bit like a game of charades, only they do not realize they are playing, and they will not jump and shout when you correctly label the dynamic at work. Instead, they will look bored or chagrined and move on to something else, which, of course, is your goal. By the way, just to complicate things even more, as you are attempting to decode their conduct, you also must work to curb their misconduct by setting consistent and compassionate limits.

In Sam's case, his transition has likely unsettled him, weakened him, and left him a little bit vulnerable, and in that mood of exhaustion and vertiginous disorientation, he reaches out to take something that is neither his nor something his mother would ever buy for him. That is, he does something he would not ordinarily do. To put it another way and far too simplistically, there's a fair chance that had Tricia gone shopping with Sam on a weekend afternoon, that chocolate bar might never have made its way into his pocket. In sum, Sam's act is more the product of situation and mood than it is an indication of a fundamental character flaw.

How Sam Loses His Integrity

Sam is out of integrity after he has stolen the chocolate bar, and, thankfully, as we would expect to observe in a five-year-old, he knows that what he has done is unquestionably wrong. This is key: his candid acknowledgment. His mom must keep this insight at the forefront of her thinking and must maintain the spotlight on her child. She must resist the impulse to disparage herself. She must also resist subscribing to the notion that he has metamorphosed overnight into a problem demon child and more than ever appreciate that he is a good, normal kid who has done a bad and abnormal thing. In other words, he has made a mistake.

We urge such parents inclined to panic to remember that "perfection" is not a reasonable expectation for a child of any age, and that, furthermore, "imperfection" is not a reflection of their parental failure. The truth is that children come to learn the value of integrity through the experience of losing it—and then through our assisting them to reestablish that integrity within themselves. Many children have shoplifted at least once in their lives, and we invite parents to conduct a search of the files in their memory's hard drive to confirm that their own experiences, or their peers', are not that dissimilar.

At the same time, shoplifting is a serious occasion, a test of our parenting and our wisdom. Realize, too, that stealing at five is one thing, while shoplifting at twelve or thirteen is quite another. (Seven and thirteen, by the way, seem to be the prime periods for shoplifting experimentation.) And shoplifting a book is different from shoplifting a pack of cigarettes, and stealing a baseball from the sporting goods store is different from stealing a pen from a classmate's desk. Every instance of stealing has unique dimensions. But if stealing becomes a pattern for older children, then we would not hesitate to say that we have other, graver concerns. Are they seeking a thrill? Are they striving to get your attention? Are they angry about living with what they perceive to be deprivation or unfair restriction? Are they stealing in the company of peers and in that way making a place for themselves in their social world? Are they repeat offenders? Certainly, if they are older and if stealing becomes a pattern despite our earnest attention, interventions, say, with a counselor, are called for because you can be sure that serious problems are preying upon them.

Still, to underscore the point when it comes to your younger children: Resist moving the heavy artillery into position. Right now your job is to help your child learn from the error so as to never repeat such an act, which means, as a practical matter, keeping your child's attention securely focused on personal integrity. Believe it or not, unless there is something deeply skewed with Sam, unless he has been terribly damaged, this is not that difficult a proposition.

But before Tricia can focus on his integrity, her primary task is, perhaps surprisingly, to take care of herself. She is going to experience multiple, conflicting emotions once she realizes that Sam has stolen something—and not just anything, either, but a candy bar, which carries additional connotations in their household. (Remember, Tricia has gone to great lengths to avoid sweets and provide nutritious foods for both herself and Sam.) Her best bet, therefore, is to make some time for herself and her self-reflections. This is the perfect moment to ask Sam to go to his room for a while, until she can collect her thoughts to speak with him about the candy bar. This is a grown-up time-out.

In general, time-outs are useful when children are no longer able to use their words to express their needs. It is not a punishment, but it is a way to discourage lashing out verbally or physically. It's also a time when they should be able to be quietly off by themselves. (Some families do not allow their children toys during a time-out, and other families allow one or two small distractions. Whatever you decide, keep it consistent.) This is similar to what Tricia needs right now. Her time-out is an acknowledgment and a practical means of taking care of herself.

On her own, she focuses centrally on two questions: Why did Sam take the candy bar? And, why now?

Unless Sam has a history of swiping things, his theft is probably attributable to his still ongoing transition to school. Sure, he can handle drop-offs, seems to enjoy the days in kindergarten, and is happy playing with his friends on the playground, but that does not mean that the transition is yet complete. In some ways, he is hanging on by his fingernails. He works hard all day to settle into the new routine, which means he lets his defenses down as soon as he is back to his old and more familiar settings—driving home with Mom or picking up dinner at the grocery store. That is, the difficulties he experienced on that first day of kindergarten have not gone away entirely. Yes, they are diminished and pushed to the edges of his awareness, but they creep back in the in-betweenness of the transitions. Once he lets his guard down, doubts surface and fatigue factors in, and in that frame of mind, he takes the stage for his acting out. In practical terms, then, it will take Sam a few more weeks, or months, for him to feel acclimated to kindergarten.

Plain and simple, Sam lost his bearings while he was in the store. He acted on his impulse to feast on the doubly forbidden fruit. And yet, though it may seem odd, by taking something, by flouting his mother's wishes, and by disappointing himself, he is trying to fill the void between the two worlds of home and school with the temporary consolation of a chocolate bar. We would be pressed to locate a conscious thought pattern. Nonetheless, starting school, he has witnessed his world turned topsy-turvy. Daily, he is doing and seeing things he never conceived possible before. He witnesses other children who do not share, some who ignore an adult's request, some who tease on the playground, and some who eat candy bars at lunch. Even if Sam had attended preschool and played with other kids in the neighborhood whose houses he frequented, kindergarten, the formal beginning of school, is still a quantum leap.

As a result of his eye-opening experiences, he revisits all his assumptions about what constitutes normal. In this state, he wonders if he can now behave differently in a store, and if he can steal a candy bar. He answers the question by acting: Yes, he can steal a candy bar, because he just did. And Tricia needs to respond: Yes, you can steal the candy bar, and you shouldn't.

Why a candy bar? The answer is a further question: Why *not* a candy bar? Sam is taking a flyer, to see what it is like to go against his mom. What is it like to eat a chocolate bar? What will it feel like and how will she respond? But of course he can never articulate this material. Tricia has to figure this out on her own before determining the natural consequence of his misbehavior—and she also needs to remember what it's like to be five.

Five Is the Age of In

Five is a wonderful age. Five is when children are into everything. In school. In the playground. In your hair. They have one speed, totally immersed in whatever they are doing.[1]

While five-year-olds are more serious than they were at four, they still seem relatively open, light-hearted, and carefree. They love to play; they *live* to play. Riding bikes, dressing up, running around the table with the dog, making up tall tales (winking to let you know that they're joking), unwilling to leave the swimming pool even when their teeth are chattering, too busy to stop for a sandwich—living in the now like this can make their parents yearn for a daily nap. For themselves and for their children.

At the same time, a five-year-old stands ready to attend to your considered opinion. Maybe that slide is a little on the scary side. Maybe that favorite coat isn't really called for on the spring day. Maybe tuna fish tastes pretty good if you give it half a chance. That's why they are drawn to the authority and nurturing of their teachers, and they will quote their wisdom about frogs and stars and sharing whenever they get the opportunity to do so.

With all this in mind about Sam, then, Tricia can proceed with confidence to the next stage of the conversation. Sam is ready to listen: He's five.

The Integrity Conversation

Sure, Tricia might ask Sam directly why he stole the candy bar, and nobody would be surprised if she did. At the same time, though, knowing the world of a five-year-old, Tricia realizes that asking *why* is more for her than for him: No five-year-old can answer that question. She needs, on her own, to connect the rest of his day to this event. The theft of the candy bar did not happen in isolation; instead, it is a part of who Sam is and what Sam does—with his mom, at school, with his friends, and on his own. Now her questions take a new slant. *Do some of the kids you have lunch with at school eat candy? Has anyone ever made fun of your lunch? Could I have handled it better in the car when you said you wanted a candy bar from the store? Who was that kid you were playing with on the playground after school? Is he a friend? Who else do you play with at school?*

It is possible that the kid he was playing with had made fun of Sam for saying no to candy at lunch one day and, in response, Sam stole the candy as an oblique way of connecting with him. Whatever the reason, Tricia will have a better understanding after listening to Sam's responses to these types of questions. After that, she is free to focus on Sam's integrity.

Now Tricia's questions take another slant. *How did it feel to take the candy without paying or without asking me? Was there a part of you that was telling you not to do it? What did it say? How did you ignore it? What did it feel like to ignore that part of yourself? How did you think I felt when I saw the candy wrapper on the sofa? How did you feel?* Hearing questions like these—getting in the habit of asking these big-picture questions—is more important, right now, than answering them. So, however Sam responds—and he, even at five, will respond—Tricia needs to end this discussion along these lines:

> Sam, this may sound weird, but I am happy that you feel so bad about taking that candy bar. This is what we have talked about before—integrity. About being true to yourself and what you know to be right. You ignored that part of you in the store today, and that worries me. But that you feel bad makes me feel better because that makes it more difficult for you to ignore your integrity in the future. But now we have to figure out how to respond to what you did.

Integrity and Consequences

Sam learns what it feels like to be out of integrity and what the implications of his being out of integrity are, when his mom speaks to him with the goal of his learning to value his wholeness. But this is not quite enough. If she were to stop here, Sam would learn about integrity, yes, but he would also be feeling guilty with no outlet for these remorseful feelings. Ultimately, he may even learn to feel bad when he does wrong without ever learning how not to do wrong in the first place. Therefore, part of Tricia's job is to give him the means to resolve his feelings of guilt.

In other words, Sam must experience natural consequences for his actions. In his case, the consequences should enable Sam to work through the guilt, restore his integrity, and, over time and not instantly, be free of his past. That is, through the administration of consequences (which follow the conversations with his mom), he can resolve this stealing incident and deepen his conception of the meaning of his action in the past, which frees him to value integrity and be guilt-free in the present. To put it another way, he needs to do something to make himself and the world whole again. Kids get this. They respect the obligation to return the toy they "borrowed," to apologize to the friend whose feelings they hurt, to make the wrong right and to make themselves and others whole again. As we shall see, Mom eventually comes up with one such workable, and visionary, solution.

However Tricia proceeds with Sam, she must figure out some consequence that invites Sam to take responsibility for his actions and to work through the guilt of his transgression. Doing so, even considering his young age, she also equips her son to deal with the still more complicated and challenging choices and decisions down the road. That's why it is never too early to put the spotlight on integrity. In the future, our children can reference these tough times, and, just as important, those resolutions as well, thereby reducing the prospects for making new mistakes and for repeating old ones.

Punishment Versus Discipline

There is an enormous difference between punishment and discipline. To punish is to impose a penalty for wrongdoing. In this sense, punishment has no interest in reparations, only in reprimanding someone. Some believe that punishment, stern and effective, will deter future misbehaviors. (If this were absolutely true, prisons would be ghost towns. Yes, there are sound justifications for putting criminals away, but the main ones are to safeguard the larger community and to rehabilitate.) If our consequences merely consist of punishment, our children will learn precious little. Perhaps they do learn how to avoid being caught, but they will not connect their misdeed to their integrity. In fact, punishment has as its main object compliance and fear, and in this way it promotes neither wisdom nor growth, but bitterness and resentment. These emotions will not deter wrongdoing.

Discipline, on the other hand, is about integrity and about fostering growth in the present *and* the future. It has the intent of correcting the behavior and inspiring a better way of acting and a more just way of being. Discipline, then, as the word's etymology suggests, has to do with being a pupil, a disciple; discipline is, therefore, essentially education, which also means at its root *guiding*.

As we come up with consequences for our children's misbehaviors, one prevailing question will help us differentiate between punishment and discipline: "Is the consequence going to teach them about how to act with integrity in the future?" If your response insists that your children take responsibility for their actions, then you are on the mark. If, however, your response merely penalizes your children while forging no connection to their integrity, you have missed an opportunity.

Throughout this book, we give numerous examples of the difference between punishment and discipline, as well as examples of appropriate consequences, but let's emphasize two here: spanking and time-outs. Spanking is always a form of punishment; children learn from being spanked that you are capable of hurting them when you get angry enough, and they will also learn to fear you. Time-outs can also constitute punishment if used improperly: "Go to your room, sit on the bed, and don't touch anything until I come up and get you." But used well, a time-out can be an appropriate and refreshing tool of discipline, of education: "I can't hear you when you're crying like this, so please take a time-out in your room for a little while to get control of yourself again.

You can play quietly with your things if you like, just calm your-self down so we can talk with one another again." This serves the same function—breaking a negative behavior pattern—but does so in a way that communicates that you believe your child is ca-pable of doing better.

A Few Words in Praise of Parental Guilt

Here are the few good words: Don't get stuck in your guilt. We know you will have your guilt. It's part of being a good parent. The other part of being a good parent is that guilt is not enough. If you wallow in guilt, you will be passive, and a passive parent is the last thing a child needs.

When your child is caught stealing, cheating, teasing, lying, or engaging in any of the other seven deadly sins of childhood, your first response, after your initial anger, will be horror and self-recrimination. Most of us look into the mirror and search for where we went wrong—as in, it must be something I did or said, or some-thing I didn't do or didn't say. Fortunately, most of us are able to separate the fiction (how our perfection might guarantee the same in our children) from the fact (children make mistakes regardless of upbringing).

If you are a single parent, however, this distinction is not so straightforward. Single parents never forget that they are alone, and among other assumptions, they feel guilty for this. The guilt a single parent feels when his or her child does something wrong taps into a deeper guilt, the guilt of being a single parent.

The other way to view the transgressions of our children is that even though such behaviors may mirror our darker sides, or so we fear, they also give us an opportunity. At this point, guilt spurs *us* on to self-punishment or self-discipline, for now we can make the linkages between suffering and disappointment, between failure and desire—only in this case, these are our feelings, too. In this way, in our attempt to salvage our children's integrity, we reaffirm our own. If role modeling means anything, it means that.

EMPTY POCKET

"That must be the person in charge," Tricia said to Sam about the imposing man wearing the white shirt and tie, two aisles away. "You ready to be a big boy, Sam?"

Sam was speechless, but his mom got down on one knee and looked him in the eye until he looked back and then said, "You can do it. I'm right here."

Sam somehow communicated to her that it was OK.

"Let's go, Sam."

Tricia introduced herself and her son to the man. She reached out and shook his hand. He said it was nice to meet her and told them that he was the manager of the grocery store. Then he turned to Sam and shook his hand, too.

"Sam has something he needs to speak with you about."

"How can I help you, Sam?"

"Yesterday I took your candy bar."

"Did you bring it back?"

"I ate it."

"You did? Without your mom paying? You know, I wondered what happened to that candy bar. I heard it was a chocolate bar. How come you did that, Sam?"

"My mom never buys them for me."

"Do you always just take things you want? I mean, do you just take your friends' things without asking them?"

Sam was staring at the floor and leaning against his mom. "No."

"I'm glad to hear that. Do you understand that it's wrong to take things from a store without asking your mom to pay for them?"

"I promise I won't do it again."

"I'm glad to hear that, too. But what are we going to do now? You still need to pay us for the candy bar."

"I don't have money."

"Well, now, we'll just have to think of something, won't we? I've got it. How about you help me unpack and stack that box of paper towels over there? That way you can work off what you owe."

Sam looked surprised, but nodded.

"OK then. Does your mom have time to wait while you help me out?"

"I'm happy to wait," she volunteered. And as the manager and Sam headed down the aisle, Tricia caught his attention and mouthed, "Thank you." She hadn't felt completely sure before, but now it felt right, making the store whole once again, helping Sam realize the personal cost of his action.

He smiled and whispered to her so that Sam, who was heading toward his job, couldn't hear: "Thanks for the call."

Tricia was pleased to see how eager Sam was to help. Yes, she was always helplessly in love with her child, helplessly proud of him as he made amends, even when he caused her momentary heartache, and somehow it made the last twenty-four hours worth it. In the next second, she headed off to the adjacent aisle, where she was going to splurge on some luxurious bath salts.

two

The Reality of Santa Claus

How Does a Child's Integrity Flower in Enchantment?

> At one time most of my friends could hear the [sleigh] bell, but as years passed, it fell silent for all of them . . . Though I've grown old, the bell still rings for me as it does for all who truly believe.
>
> —**Chris Van Allsburg,** *The Polar Express*

IS HE STILL COMING TO TOWN?

—One—

When Tom came through the door with Tanya after Saturday afternoon errands, Celeste could instantly sense that something was not quite right. She gave her husband a "What happened now?" glance, and he replied by raising his eyebrows, universal spousal sign language for "We have to talk."

"Mommy!" Tanya cried out and came over to her mom for a hug and an arm squeeze and a head scratch, which made the six-year-old giggle a little before squirming away and bouncing around the room for the next ten seconds, between toys and the cat and her stash of favorite books.

"Hey there, Bugaboo, I missed you," said Celeste. "You and Daddy have fun?"

"We went to the store, Mommy, and I can't tell you what Daddy and me got you for Christmas, so don't ask." Celeste turned very, very serious. "Don't snoop!"

"Sure, honey. You hungry?"

"No, but you can't snoop. Tell her she can't snoop, Daddy."

"That's right, Celeste. Snooping is not a viable option for you."

"You sure you're not hungry, sweetheart?" Celeste asked.

"No!" Tanya galloped into her room and commenced another conversation with her caged cockateel, whom she had named Smokey, who was sweetly squawking in his let-me-spread-my-wings rallying cry. Meanwhile, her parents moved into the kitchen, where they couldn't be overheard.

"OK," said Celeste, "tell me already."

"I thought six-year-olds still believed in Santa Claus," Tom said. "I read it in that book you keep on the nightstand."

Celeste winced.

"I guess it was bound to happen sooner or later. I was just counting on later, much later," he said.

"Slow down. How do you know she doesn't believe in Santa Claus?"

"That's probably overstating it. I was just talking, we were driving around, and I asked her if she finished her letter to Santa Claus. She just shrugged and was quiet and I felt this uh-oh surge in the pit of my stomach. About a minute later, she goes, 'Is there really a Santa Claus?' I asked her what made her ask such a crazy question. She said that there are a whole lot of kids for him to read all those letters and bring presents to all of them."

"So she's wondering if there's a Santa, but she worries that he's too busy to read her letter now?"

He threw up his hands.

"How the heck did that happen? You think it had something to do with you two getting me a present?"

"She can still compartmentalize. It's one thing what presents Santa drags down the chimney and another thing what presents we get each other. But here's the kicker. It seems that she heard some older kids in the courtyard, during recess—"

"That's another reason big kids should be kept away from first-graders."

"I agree, but anyway. Some kid said something to her, or maybe she overheard something—it's all unclear to me—about how there was no Santa Claus. About how only babies think there's a Santa Claus."

"So what did you tell her, Dr. Spock, when she asked if there was a Santa Claus?"

"What do you think, Celeste? I said, 'Of course there is a Santa Claus.'"

"You what! You lied to her?"

Tom shrugged.

"That'll come back to us in a few years. How'd she respond?"

"Hard to tell. She kept looking out the window. 'Look at that dog, Daddy, that's a fire-engine dog. Can we get one?' If I had to bet, I'd say she felt relieved when I told her there was a Santa."

Celeste sighed and folded her arms and leaned back against the kitchen counter.

Tom said, "Now what should we do?"

"Do we tell her that there is no Santa Claus or do we stick to a white lie? Both of those make me nervous."

"It doesn't feel like a lie to me. What is the truth about Santa Claus? I mean, does he have to exist to be real?"

"She's six years old, Tom. Don't you think we can hold the line for one more year? Doesn't she deserve that much? At this rate, next thing we know, she'll be going to the senior prom."

"I think we have a ways to go until that event, and besides, we'll be driving her and her date, right?"

"I don't think she's ready to date."

"Daughters are never ready to date," Tom said.

"My mom thought I wasn't ready to date yet and that was when I told her I was marrying you."

"Sometimes, my mother-in-law shocks me with her insight into her prize possession."

—Two—

At the end of dinner that night, Tom served up his celebrated dessert: bread pudding. He always made the same dramatic presentation: "And now, the specialty of the maison la casa house. Ta da." Actually, it was the only dessert he knew how to make, and despite the kudos that streamed his way every time, he never experimented with other desserts. After all, bread pudding was a life's work. It took a commitment to perfect a bread budding, he figured, and he was ready to rise to the challenge.

"Like your dessert, honey?" Celeste asked her daughter.

Tanya nodded, offering nothing besides an *Mmmmm* that accompanied her slow and methodical spoon. She was a very precise eater these days. Suddenly, it seemed very, very long ago that the cat and the dog had skulked under her high chair with absolute confidence that treats would come their way if they were patient. Tanya was also a little quieter than normal tonight.

"Good job, Tom, as always."

"At this time I would like to thank the little people that made my dessert possible. Stale bread—that is the secret."

"Your daddy's pretty silly, isn't he?"

Tanya nodded again and smiled a little. Smokey was trilling his life away in the distance.

"Ah," said Tom, "what would a house be without a parakeet?"

"Quiet?" asked Celeste.

"Smokey's not a parakeet," said Tanya very defiantly. "He's a cockateel."

"You're right, sweetheart," said her mom, picking up on Tanya's suddenly faintly snarky mood. "He certainly is a cockateel, a very loud cockateel, and we all love him."

"Changing subjects," announced Tom. "Celeste, have *you* finished *your* letter to Santa Claus?"

Celeste quizzed him with her eyes. She didn't know where this was going yet. "I'm not sure. Have I?"

Tanya stopped chewing and sat back in the chair, as if she wanted to listen more closely.

"Have you been good, Celeste?" said Tom.

"Yeah, Mommy, have you been good? That's what Santa needs to know."

"Not as good as you, Tanya, but I have been very good."

"Would you like a second opinion?" asked Tom.

"Not particularly. But Tanya, did you finish your letter to Santa today?"

"Uh-huh."

"That's nice," said Celeste, trying to sound matter-of-fact.

But now Tanya had something to say. It came out as a sort of question, however, and it was directed at both her parents. "Santa is coming soon."

Her mother agreed and then asked her daughter what she wanted from Santa this year.

Tanya proclaimed with absolute resolution that she wanted a Shetland pony, a computer, a soccer ball, and this blue dress she saw today with Daddy. She had certainly thought it all through before now. They had seen a team of Shetland ponies at a parade last summer. Tanya seemed taken by them at the time, but she had never given a clue that they were still on her mind.

"What's your number one favorite present idea for Santa?" asked Tom raptly, hoping that Tanya was going to give him and Santa something semipractical to work with. *Please, don't say pony,* he thought to himself.

Clearly, Tanya had thought this through as well. Her number one favorite was a computer. Her other number one favorite was also a computer.

Celeste and Tom both sagged in their dinner-table chairs, sharing in the comfort that it wasn't the pony after all. Which was very fortuitous, because this year more than ever before, Santa needed to deliver the right stuff.

Then Tanya said, "Daddy, have *you* written Santa yet?"

"Glad you asked me, Tee. I'm thirty-seven," Tom remarked.

Tanya observed that that was indeed a very big number.

"That's right, I am very old, and I'm still counting on Santa and he's never let me down."

"Daddy, don't listen," said Tanya, and he covered his mouth with both hands. "Close your ears, I said!" He complied. Then she slipped from her chair and whispered into her mommy's ear through her cupped little hands.

"Really, Ya?" said Celeste.

"Really!" she whispered loud enough for Smokey to hear. Then Tanya scampered out of the room and ran outside through the back door.

"Get good and muddy!" cried Tom.

"Silly Daddy," Tanya giggled.

"What's the big secret?" Tom wanted to know once the coast was clear.

"The girl knows what you want for Christmas."

"A sports car?"

"You haven't been good enough for Santa to break his budget for you, buster. But Tanya knows what you want. You want that panda bear you two admired in Mister Oatmeal's Toys this afternoon."

"You know, it was a pretty cute little bear."

"There, that wasn't so bad. I think Santa lives for another year."

NOTES HOME

Integrity is not a black-and-white, either-or category. It's more comprehensive than sticking to the facts, and along the path of your child's development, integrity will wear a changing face. If it weren't so, supporting your two-year-old's belief in Santa Claus would be tantamount to lying. After all, when you give your child the idea of Santa Claus, you are giving a wonderful gift. Strictly speaking, of course, it's tantamount to an untruth, but that doesn't make it any less beautiful. And as the poet John Keats wrote, "Beauty is truth, truth beauty."

Children travel all the time between the realms of fantasy and reality, hardly pausing, much less noticing, the boundaries. And because integrity, as we have said, is about being whole, children need to live in each and both worlds—and we need to support them as they do. In this twilight world, imaginary friends can take up residence. Dolls and toy figures can make for lots of conversation. Pretend-dragons can require food and walking. Characters in books can feel as important as siblings or parents. There is a tremendous upside to these relationships. For one thing, children learn how to be alone without being lonely. More specifically, with an imaginary friend, for instance, children practice empathy. With dolls, they rehearse the nuances of social interaction and good manners. With pretend-dragons, they experience the joy of caretaking. With books, they exercise the powers of their imagination, which is, as we will see, deeply connected to their moral lives.

So *how* do we support them? We follow their lead and play along with the existence of an imaginary friend, therefore, and our play and theirs will merge in the endorsement of a rich and beautiful double world that is made up of both fantasy and reality. And *why* do we support them? Because being alone, empathy, social consciousness, joy, and imagination are the hallmarks of integrity.

We must continually update our expectations of our children, depending on their age and their shifting psychological and emotional needs. In a way, this reminds us of the old joke: Little Johnny goes to his mom and says, "Where did I come from?" Mom gulps and, once she regains her composure, tells the story about swimmers and eggs and so on. After a long time, Johnny looks up, mystified, and says, "That's not where my friend comes from."

"No?"

"No, he says he came from Ohio."

In other words, listen to what your kids are really asking when they zero in about Santa Claus or any other important issue. And also be aware of *who* they are when they are asking.

Is There Really a Santa Claus?

Depends on whom you ask. Pose the question to a typical four-year-old and you will get an answer in the affirmative without a moment's hesitation. The child would also probably stare in disbelief at the absurdity of the question. (And you can count on some crazy uncle or distant cousin to make the inquiry.) Ask teenagers and they will shake their head in equal incredulity, and probably not even grace you with a response.

The answer also depends on who is asking. If it is your three-year-old, you say yes, and if it is your fifteen-year-old, well, a serious conversation on the topic is long overdue.

In the case of Santa Claus, for a younger child, *belief* in him makes the child whole. As children grow older, however, their integrity will lead them to question and then deny his existence. That is why, for an older child, *doubt* in Santa makes the child whole.

At five, some children have an inkling as to the fiction of Santa Claus but gloss over it as swiftly as possible. To a lesser extent, the same is true at six. At seven and eight, things change. These children begin to believe that there probably is no Santa Claus, but just in case they are wrong, they are more than willing to continue with their rituals of writing out a list for Santa and leaving cookies and milk out on Christmas Eve. By nine, most kids are certain that Santa does not exist and easily move into the realm of gift giving as an exchange between family members who love one another. This is the birth of the spirit of giving during the holiday season.

Tanya is six, which means she is on the front end of questioning the plausibility of Santa but a long way from giving up her precious belief in him. That is, she is both a believer and a nonbeliever. In her heart, she knows there is a Santa Claus and cannot imagine ever giving up that thought. In her head, though, she is beginning to consider what the older kids are saying. She is also capable, in a cognitive way, of sorting through fact and fiction. Between six and eight, most children come to realize that the simple logistics of Santa's visiting every house in the world in one night loaded with presents for each and every family amounts to an impossibility. (In other words, they can live with contradiction and can believe both that there is no Santa and that he is bringing me the wonderful presents I asked for.) When they put this together, however, they will not turn to you for affirmation of this insight. This all happens quietly, off to the side (though this is also the time that some may force their new understanding on younger children, which we will address in a later "Note Home" in this chapter).

At this age, children can live in two different worlds, worlds that to adults appear mutually exclusive. Tanya can live in a world where Santa Claus visits every home on the planet while simultaneously wondering how the heck this is possible, which is why she can Christmas shop with her dad and trust that Santa will come to her house, too. This is healthy. Enjoy the moment while it lasts.

Fantasy and Reality Don't Conflict

These early years of childhood are rich in imagination, fantasy, and play. This is when your son in solitary will play baseball for hours in the backyard, role-playing different players on competing teams, commenting on the action in his role as radio announcer, and cheering and booing alternately, a member of both the home and visiting crowds. Or this is when your daughter will have a formal tea party with her four favorite dolls on the floor of her bedroom, complete with cups and saucers, conversation, disagreements, apologies, laughter, and good-byes. There is nothing wrong with any of this; indeed, the absence of an active imagination and fantasy life at this age is reason for legitimate worry.

Children are able to mesh fantasy and reality more easily than most adults realize. Just look at the phenomenally successful television show *Sesame Street*. According to author Malcolm Gladwell in *The Tipping Point*, the producers of the show originally had Muppets exclusively interacting with other Muppets and people interacting exclusively with people.[1] They went to great efforts not to mix Muppets with real people for fear of confusing reality and fantasy in child viewers—a view that many research psychologists supported. What they discovered, however, was that kids were initially not all that interested in the show: They were engrossed by the Muppets, but whenever the Muppets were absent and people dominated the scene, their attention strayed. As soon as Muppets interacted directly with people, however, the kids were riveted. To date, there has been no research that has shown this type of mixed reality and fantasy to be even remotely problematic in children's development. The lesson we learn from this example is that for kids, fantasy and reality not only overlap nicely but also support and reinforce each other. This melding of fantasy and reality is going to play out through the next few years, sometimes very dramatically when some eight-year-olds, for instance, may well cultivate imaginary friends, with whom they will have rich and interesting relationships.

Being Six Years Old

Six is a tricky age. Most six-year-olds live at the extremes, and in this regard they are not all that different from two-and-a-half-year-olds—thus their frequent flip-flops and swings among clashing desires, opinions, and moods. They are ambivalent about a great many things. This is a time when kids do things that they have never done before: breaking into tears at the slightest provocation, refusing to lie still in bed at night, and generally wreaking havoc with morning routines. In part, these changes stem from their growing independence. This is why, at times, they can push their parents away so harshly, and why, in the next moment, they are seeking reassurances that they are indeed good boys and girls. Six is a vulnerable year (for parents, too).[2]

This is the age when parents get their first real inkling into the split personality of their child—a child who can be a terror at home while at the same time a joy at school. (For every parent, this is important to appreciate and never to forget. Now is the time to get in the habit of asking and listening to what teachers say about your child. This insight, that the child is well behaved elsewhere, is a kind of consolation at home, where that same child can be anything but well behaved and manageable.) Meanwhile, at school, friends are more important than ever, even though most six-year-olds are combative and unforgiving of one another, and even though they are mercurial in their allegiances to one another. Sarah can be your daughter's best friend on Tuesday and then be ignored on Wednesday, when Sheila vaults ahead, only to be reinstated on Friday.

Six is a creative year, marked by strong needs to express creativity through whatever means available: drawing, playing, reading, singing. This is when kids take advantage of every occasion, too. They might break into song at the movie theater. They might delete a few files on your computer if it interferes with a game they are playing. Suddenly there's no difference between a nice white wall and an easel. Stock up on supplies. It is almost as if your child wants to scream out at least once a day: "Look at me! Aren't I wonderful?"

Physically, most six-year-olds are restless. In this regard, if your child is in a first grade that requires lots of sitting, expect bountiful energy and activity after school. (You should also consider talking to the teacher and urging more active outlets during the day.) It's helpful to recall the teachings of Jean Piaget, who wrote beautifully about the bustling brain of a child, about how thought is action, and action is motion, and motion is thought. Next time you see your six-year-old tearing through the house (probably with a big smile on her face, while you are urging her to "Slow down!"), perhaps you might reflect that she is simply working out, and celebrating, everything she is and is becoming. (You might also find another location for the expensive vase.)

Parents' Integrity in Both Worlds

The question is not whether there is a Santa Claus or not, it is what to say when your six- to eight-year-old child asks you about it. And this is what Celeste and Tom face when Tanya raises the topic while out Christmas shopping with her dad. But before we go further, let's be clear about one important point: No parent is prepared for this moment when it happens. Even if you and your spouse have talked about it; even if you have rehearsed your response in your head; even if you have committed this chapter to memory—this conversation catches every parent by surprise. No parents are ready to see their children growing up this fast—we all have a tendency to want to keep them just a bit younger than they are. This initial doubt as to Santa Claus is one of those archetypal moments in every family's life.

What is essential in your response to these queries is grasping what is at play here and appreciating the deeper questions your child is addressing.

When it comes to *Sesame Street* and to Santa Claus, the job of parents is not to assert factual reality but, instead, to affirm their children's need to thrive in different worlds simultaneously. In practical terms, this means that integrity is not always predicated 100 percent of the time upon truth and honesty. In the formation of character, sometimes a so-called fact needs to take a back seat to imagination and play. Simply put, Tanya's underlying question is not *about* Santa Claus but rather about Mom, Dad, and family. To her, the question feels something like this: "Do Mommy and Daddy know how to take care of me? And will they?" For Tanya, therefore, the deeper issue has to do with her relationships with those she loves and those who love her—the very people who constitute her connection to her world. Her parents have until now given her shelter, sustenance, love, laughter, knowledge, experience, guidance—and Santa Claus. If they take away Santa, what else may follow? And that means that her central question boils down to a matter of trust and security. Can she trust her parents to give her what she needs in moments of crisis?

What all six-year-olds entertaining unsettling doubts about Santa Claus need are compassionate, imaginative parents who will follow their lead in facing their confusion. At the same time, these parents need to be more than neutral. When Tanya is six, they ought be more supportive of the belief in Santa Claus, whereas when she is eight, they will be less supportive of the fantasy, but not too supportive of the truth, either. Tanya needs her parents to hear her doubts about Santa, but not surrender to them. At the same time they cannot lie, either, because those are the kinds of lies that come back to erode the foundation of parents' relationships with their children down the road—and sometimes, not too far down the road.

This is not that complicated to accomplish. It means listening to your child's doubts without agreeing or disagreeing. It means putting out milk and cookies for Santa and carrots for his reindeer. It means putting presents under the tree with a "From Santa" tag attached. It means doing all this even if your daughter is looking less than completely certain. Emotionally, however, this is about as complex as it gets—for it means nothing less than watching as your daughter struggles to figure out what she believes. It means listening as she tells you what the older kids are saying about Santa, despite your best efforts to protect her from this sort of disappointment. It means looking at her in a manner that conveys "You'll figure it out, honey. And even if you come to a conclusion you prefer not to reach, you'll be OK. In fact, you'll be better for having gone through this struggle."

Pragmatically, this translates into Tom and Celeste's doing everything in their power, short of lying, to support Tanya's wish for the existence of Santa Claus. Therefore, Tom takes a misstep when he categorically denies Santa's nonexistence. This is not a fatal error, but we can count on this topic coming up again, a few years down the road. The point here is that parents make mistakes because they love their kids and will do and say anything to prevent or assuage their pain, in the short term.

So how do we respond to a six-year-old's direct question?

—Daddy, is there a Santa Claus?
—What makes you think there is no Santa Claus?
—It's an awful big world to go around in one night.
—It is a big world. But you believe in magic, don't you? I do. That's where you came from. And you bring magic into my life every day.

In the best of all worlds, parents provide triage for Santa and life support for Tanya's faith. She will pull the plug on this mechanism of assistance when she is ready, and not sooner. But her parents will not know the moment that she pulls the plug on her belief because, remember, she will still be going through the family rituals *as if she still believed*. On this one, kids would much rather be safe than sorry. (In a sense, she may hold on to her belief a while longer in order to take care of her parents, who, she believes, still wish to see their daughter subscribing to his existence. This is another instance of her ability to live a fiction and to merge the reality and fantasy of a family life.) And that's why the first Christmas Tanya's parents realize she does not believe in Santa will be tinged with both sadness and wonder that their little girl is growing up. So, finally, do not rush yourself or the search for the answer to the question. To respect the question means to respect the questioner, and that is the key to sustaining our own integrity and, of course, to instilling a sense of it in our children.

Imagination and Success

Play and imagination are not digressions or detours away from reality but the essential bridges to reality. As parents, we must never forget this, whether our child is six or sixteen. Yes, a few children can get lost in their own world, but very few do. Many more get thrust into reality before play and imagination have had the time, sunshine, and space to build a bridge strong enough to handle the many comings and goings between play and imagination on one side of the ravine of their experience and reality on the other.

When we say we want to prepare our children for reality, don't we mean we want them to be responsible, to enjoy healthy relationships with peers and adults, to be alert to the risks and opportunities that life provides? Yet it was the poet William Butler Yeats who wrote, "In dreams begin responsibilities." Responsibilities grow out of an active imagination, in other words, not out of a failure of imagination.

A superficial conception of responsibility suggests that adults have order, continuity, follow-through, and all the tools that seemingly enable somebody to navigate the so-called real world. Those tools are valuable, no doubt, but every triumphant breakthrough in business, art, politics, or anywhere else important is accomplished by those who love their work and see things that nobody else can see. For them, play and work are not that different. If you ask a writer whether he is working or playing when he is writing a story, he will likely regard the question as slightly meaningless. Or if you ask a litigator whether she is working or playing when she is making her closing arguments, she will have trouble making the distinction. The same quandary applies to architects designing a building, to criminal investigators tracking down clues, to doctors making a diagnosis, to teachers asking the right question. If you want to see where productive adults come from, look at kids in sandboxes, scratching away at poems, singing new songs, talking to their dolls, baking cookies for Santa Claus on Christmas Eve.

Lamentably, some of us try to push our kids ahead, to make sure that they are better than average, to have them be accepted into programs for the gifted and talented at their elementary schools. Sometimes that is the appropriate path for that child, but more often these paths seem attractive because the parents wish to feel better about themselves. Somehow, we erroneously assume that "bright" children inevitably grow into healthy adults. But it's just not so. Children need to be children, and what comes most naturally to children is play and imagination. They are not little adults. Therefore, we cannot treat them as if they were.

Bruno Bettelheim, the eminent author and child psychologist, believed that a childhood deficient in play and imagination made for an adulthood susceptible to cults, fads, and fringe belief systems.[3] That is, when restricting reality is pressed upon children quickly and autocratically, they become adults less confident dealing with the eventual contingencies of everyday adult life. The more we as parents can encourage explorative play and flights of imagination, the healthier and happier our kids will be. Interestingly, doing so, they will also stand a better chance of becoming more motivated teenagers and more successful adults. Above all, encouraging explorative play and flights of imagination will help a child build a healthy sense of integrity.

Older Siblings and Older Children

When you learn that your children have heard from older kids that Santa Claus does not exist—that only babies believe in Santa Claus—take a few deep breaths. And stop to remember that in a few years, at nine or ten, your child will be the one telling younger children the same thing. That's the nature of the developing child. This is also a good time to pay attention to your own integrity.

Yes, you will be angry that these older children have forced your daughter or son to deal with something that she or he is too young to make sense out of. But your frustration will not help her one bit. Nor will your earnest assertion that they are wrong, because you "know" for a fact that there is a Santa Claus. Sure, this will help in the moment, but in a year or two she will not have forgotten that you lied to her—that, in her mind, you treated her like a little child. For similar reasons, you back yourself into a corner if you counter by expressing your absolute belief in Santa Claus. Your best bet is again to listen to what she says. Hear her out. Perhaps you might express empathy for the older kids: "Isn't it sad that they don't believe in Santa Claus?" Most five- and six-year-olds will nod in agreement, make a few empathetic comments of their own, and move on to another subject. Then it's your job to continue with the holiday rituals because children need these customs to sweep them back into the spirit of the holiday.

When you have one child who still believes in Santa and another who has crossed the threshold, you have a wonderful opportunity at hand. This is the time again to support both worlds: the reality of your older child and both worlds of your younger one. Pull the older one aside and explain how you know she is a big girl and understands that there is no "real" Santa, but that you need her help. She will glow at the prospect of real responsibility and the idea of your needing her. Explain that her younger sibling still believes, and that this is a good thing, just as it was when she was that age. Then ask her to help you support his belief in Santa. Give her some practical suggestions: Write your letters to Santa together, bake the cookies for Christmas Eve together. Quickly, she will get the idea and start coming up with her own ideas. The key is to give her a role in supporting his belief in Santa, because without that clarity she is likely to undermine his sense of enchantment as a way of asserting her own "big-girlness." The responsibility you assign her gives her another avenue she can follow to demonstrate both maturity and love.

Anti-Bah-Humbug

As children grow up, and become conscious of growing up, they gradually cast off the garments of their former thinking. They hate being thought of as a "baby," and they see around them that their peers are suddenly confused if not downright skeptical about Santa. Here is the beauty of childhood: It is about *and*, not *either-or*. As parents, we need to feel this deep in our bones; otherwise, we risk infantilizing our children just when they need us to support their growth or forcing reality upon them before they are ready.

Consider six-year-olds' grasp of the concept of death. When faced with the loss of someone they know, most children this age will wrestle openly with the permanence of death. Strangely, they seem—if we go by their statements on the subject—to get this quickly. "Uncle Ernesto is dead, so he isn't alive anymore. That's why we are having a funeral for him." But listen a bit longer and you hear the other side of that understanding. "Mommy, when will Uncle Ernesto come to dinner again?" This is the child's world, which is more encompassing than most adults' worlds. And it is only through living in both worlds that Tanya can remain whole, which is what integrity is all about.

Tanya's Christmas, This Year

Tanya has this year, and possibly next, to hold on to her fantasy of Santa Claus and his reindeer coming to her house on Christmas Eve. For her parents, of course, this is a major awakening, and they will feel a little sad and a little protective about her, realizing that some of her precious childhood has slipped away. More than any Christmas before, now is the time for them to focus on the spirit of the holiday—giving, thankfulness, compassion, forgiveness, love— because this is a transition year. Now they have to contemplate a Christmas when Tanya no longer believes in Santa and what they want that to be like. For some kids, religion may well take on a new intensity. This is also an ideal time to invent or revitalize rituals that are enacted every season regardless of the belief in Santa—caroling around the neighborhood, volunteering at a local soup kitchen, reading books aloud as a family. In this way, the enchantment of Santa Claus is never lost or forgotten, it just takes a different form, one that is not in conflict with growing up.

Perhaps you might leave a book like *The Polar Express* by Chris Van Allsburg in your child's room, or even better, reread the book aloud together. (If you listen carefully, maybe you will hear the bell, too.) Just remember that for every child, Santa Claus (or some Santa Claus–like figure) is symbolic *and* real. He is symbolic of a beautiful philosophy and a generous spirit. And he is real because for all kids, Santa is Mom and Dad, and not just when they are children, either. In their hearts, you are Santa Claus for eternity.

three

Loss

How Does My Child Develop Integrity in Times of Sadness and Grief?

> Because I could not stop for Death—
> He kindly stopped for me—
> The Carriage held but just Ourselves—
> And Immortality.
>
> **—Emily Dickinson**

TOTO, TOO?

—One—

Corinne was an only child, and she was very serious. That's not completely right. It was when she became seven that she suddenly turned very serious, and serious about everything—school, teachers, family, her clothes, her toys, her grandparents. She looked deep and meditatively into your eyes when you said something she didn't quite comprehend or agree with. At other times, she let you know by her silences and staring into the distance that there was always a dialogue going on inside.

She was serious, and possessive, when it came to Archie, too. Archie was a mixed-breed dog getting up there in years, and

Corinne had loved him from virtually the first day she laid eyes on him in the company of Kenny, then her mom's new, special friend. And Archie, who was patient and even-tempered when it came to kids, seemed especially fond of Corinne.

It was now a little over two years ago that Archie moved in along with Kenny, who married her mom. Archie liked to sleep at night in Corinne's room and enjoyed the treats she slipped him when nobody was looking. And she was serious when it came to her responsibility for filling his water bowl and accompanying Kenny on the nightly Archie stroll.

Her parents and her stepparents were not terribly concerned about her mood shift, however; seriousness like hers, her second-grade teacher commented, was an unsurprising and often a temporary stage in development. So even though everybody kept a watchful eye on her, they tried to take her personality change in stride. In fact, from early on, her mom was pleased about Corinne's emotional connection with Archie; she had the thought that such a sweet and playful dog would provide company for her and help her grow up.

One day, while they were gathered in the kitchen before they left early for school and work that day, Corinne's mom, Leanne, told her something she had heard in her yoga class the previous night: "Corinne, you know what my teacher said?"

"What'd you hear in yogurt class, Mommy?"

"*Yoga* class. She said, 'It's OK to face your worries, but you don't have to invite them in for tea.'"

Corinne's stepdad, Kenny, couldn't stop himself. "That's pretty cool. I like that. I think it's even true."

Corinne considered at length the point and then concluded reflectively, "I don't like tea."

"Not even with milk and honey?" said Leanne.

"Little bit, with honey, when it's cold outside."

"What did the vet say about Archie?" Leanne asked Kenny.

Kenny sighed and rolled his sad eyes in Corinne's direction, as if to tell his wife, "Not now."

That same night, picking a moment when Corinne bustled out of the room, Kenny told his wife what had happened with Archie. "Dr. Granger said we're getting closer and closer to the moment of decision."

"He actually said 'moment of decision'?"

"Didn't have to."

Leanne and Kenny had been preparing themselves for this awful inevitability, even though neither of them could quite believe it. Kenny had adopted Archie from the pound long before he had ever met Leanne, but he had been a central member of their new family from the first, only now he was twelve years old, which was at the upper limit of anybody's expectations. Archie was a forty-pound tangle of wiry graying hair, part schnauzer, part terrier, part mystery mutt, they said with affection, a bundle of energy until the last few months, when he had started sleeping more than ever and his cataractous eyes had taken on a dull, opaque appearance. Sometimes he skipped a meal or two, which was something he had never done before, and sometimes he turned up his nose at the prospect of a liver treat or a thrown tennis ball. Occasionally, when they called his name, he didn't indicate that he heard them.

"His weight's down a couple of pounds, too," Kenny said, "but he was wagging his tail when he saw everybody at the animal hospital, so that's good."

"I'm really not looking forward to this," said Leanne.

"I know, I know. Me, either. They did a blood panel, because he had a little fever, so we'll know more tomorrow. I brought home some antibiotics, and we're supposed to take it easy on him."

"We're not going to let Archie suffer, right, Kenny? If he can't enjoy his life, we owe it to him to do the right thing. He's thirteen and he's had a good life."

"Twelve, but you're right, and we'll do what we have to do. For Archie."

Leanne was concerned about what Kenny was going through and she told him so. He replied that it was going to break his heart, but he had to do right by Archie. They also agreed that they needed to keep Corinne in focus throughout, because she was going to be devastated. They wondered how much she understood what was about to happen. "It's funny," said Kenny, "but it almost helps me to keep Corinne in mind. I'm not saying it's going to make it easier, but if I think about her, it gives me something else to think about and—"

At this point, Corinne bounded back into the room. It was twilight, the time before dinner when she and Kenny walked Archie. She had his leash in her grasp. "Where's Archie?"

"He's pretty tired, sweetheart," said Kenny. "I think we're going to let him rest tonight." Archie was asleep on their bed, in fact, something they never let him do before, but now rules like that seemed beside the point.

"I want to go for a walk with Archie. It's my turn to hold the leash tonight, Kenny."

Leanne took a deep breath. "Archie's taking some medicine, Corinne, and the doctor said we should let him rest tonight so he can feel better tomorrow."

"Does he have the flu?"

"Funny, I asked the vet that same question," said Kenny, "but you know, dogs don't get the flu. Though they do get bugs and take medicine that isn't that different from what you take."

Then Corinne looked at Kenny hard and blurted out, "Is Archie going to die?"

Leanne and Kenny were silent for a while, as they both grasped for the first time precisely how much Corinne did know, and then Leanne said, "Someday, Corinne, yes. Archie is very old."

"But he's not going to die right now, right?" said Corinne. It sounded like half a question, half a hope.

"No," said Kenny, "I doubt he'll die tonight."

"So let's go for a walk. Archie always goes for a walk."

"Doctor said he should take it easy, Corinne, so we're going to let Archie rest."

Corinne looked very disappointed. "If he can't go for a walk, I'm going to sit next to him in case he's lonely."

"That's a very good idea," said Leanne. "He'd like that. He's up in our bedroom; he'll be happy to see you."

"Kenny," said Corinne, "why don't you come on up with me to sit with Archie?"

"In a minute," he said and she replied, "OK," and went up the stairs, still holding the leash. Maybe she was planning on talking Archie into going for that walk.

"This is going to be worse than we thought," Leanne said.

"That's impossible," Kenny said. "It can't get any worse."

A few minutes later, after embracing Leanne, Kenny thought he had the strength to walk up the stairs, so he did.

–Two–

Around midnight, Corinne was tugging on her mom's nightshirt. "Mommy, my worries came in and I didn't even invite them in for tea."

Leanne sat up in bed, turned on the night-light, and held her daughter's outstretched hands. "What did your worries want from you?" she said distantly, gathering her wits.

"I don't know, but I'm worried about Archie."

"Me, too, sweetheart."

"I don't want him to be sick anymore."

"Me, either. We're going to do everything we can for him. And we'll all talk in the morning. Can I take you back to your bed?"

Corinne struggled for a second, unsure of what to say, before agreeing.

Because they didn't sleep much that night, Kenny and Leanne were a little groggy when the sun came through the kitchen window that Saturday morning. Kenny was supposed to call for the blood test results in a couple of hours. He kept looking at the clock for the time to arrive. But then the phone rang. Kenny picked up the receiver. It was the vet.

Both he and Leanne instantly had a sinking feeling.

Kenny listened intensely, and from across the room Leanne could tell the news was not encouraging. Dr. Granger always gave you lots of information, maybe too much information, and that's why his explanations took up time. This time, though, Kenny wasn't impatient. He was hanging on every word.

"Yes . . . I understand . . . So there's really nothing . . . OK . . . " There was a lot of silence, and Leanne could faintly hear Dr. Granger's sympathetic voice. After a while, ten minutes by the clock that felt like an hour, Kenny hung up the phone.

"Kenny?"

"Not good," said Kenny. Then he named the incurable blood disease Archie was suffering from. Archie was going to feel tired and listless and run down, and one day he was going to get very sick. There wasn't much to do except make Archie as comfortable as possible.

Corinne came into the kitchen and took down her bowl for cereal. "Can Archie go out today?"

Kenny was upset but he spoke calmly. "It's up to him. But if Archie wants to go for a walk, sure, we'll all go for a walk later."

But they never did go for that walk before Corinne was picked up by her dad. And that Saturday, Archie took a very bad turn. He didn't get up from his bed and paid no attention to the food or the water bowl. He looked remote and troubled.

"I don't think I can do this," said Kenny to Leanne. "When the time comes, can we go together?"

"Let's wait till Monday," Leanne suggested. "If he's still out of it, we'll—" She couldn't finish the sentence.

"What do we want to do with Corinne? How much do we tell her?"

"I think we tell her what she wants to know. Let's follow her lead. She knows more than we give her credit for."

By Sunday night, however, it was painfully obvious what they had to do the next morning. So when Corinne came back from the weekend with her dad, they sat her down to talk it through, to prepare her and to some extent themselves for Monday.

They explained that Archie was very sick and that he was not going to get better. She wanted to know how they knew this, and Kenny said that after talking with the doctor again that day, he found out what he knew all along, namely, that when a dog stops eating, drinking, and playing, he wants to go to heaven. Kenny wasn't particularly religious, and neither was Leanne, so he was surprised that he used the word, but it felt right, all the same.

"Dogs go to heaven?" Corinne almost welcomed the news, and she almost smiled.

"Yes," said Leanne, following along with Kenny, "Archie is a great dog and he gets to go to heaven, where he can play again and not be sick anymore, and where he won't even be old."

"But he's going to be lonely. We're not going to be there."

"Not for a while, sweetheart, you're right, but he'll be waiting for us when we get there."

In the next second, all three of them were in tears.

"He's going to be the best dog in heaven," said Corinne.

"You're right," said Kenny.

"Mommy, can I have some ice cream?"

"Sure."

"Can we give some to Archie? I used to give him ice cream when you weren't looking."

NOTES HOME

How Much Information Does a Child Need?

Children are blessed by their natural and insatiable curiosity, which is one reason they continually draw perceptive, attentive adults into their orbit of wonder and joy. At seven, or really at any young age, they have a question inspired by every occasion and observation. They also hang on every word you utter, even if they do not let you know it. Days, even weeks and months later, they will quote back to you something you cannot quite remember saying, and they will be—often to your shock—invariably accurate.

When children ask questions, parents can sometimes provide more information than a child needs. There is no hard-and-fast rule here, however, other than this: Listen carefully to what is being asked. Then, as well as you can, answer only the question that has been asked.

Beyond that, we are open with our kids, but open differently from how we are with our spouses and other adults who need fuller disclosure. "Are you OK, Daddy?" is a question that does not require reference to detailed financial reports or frank statements as to professional challenges or injustices. At the same time, we need to acknowledge that our children are quite savvy in their ability to read our moods, and we should not miss the chance to let them know that they are accurately reading their world, and ours. We do not want to mislead our children by burdening them with adult problems or with an overly rosy and simplistic picture of the world. Of course, human beings endure tough times. Grandparents, for instance, grow old and infirm. Sometimes we go through rough spells with our siblings and in-laws and our own parents. And one day the dogs that children love will exist no more.

What Do Death and Life Mean to a Seven-Year-Old Child?

Seven is a contemplative year, a time of searching and restless internalized wanderings. School can feel to seven-year-olds like an alien place, and their teachers seem to them to be like another species. Now, they fantasize, teachers are suddenly prone to criticize and chastise them for no reason. Injustices will rankle. Insecurities will abound. *Unfair!* will enter their working vocabulary.[1]

Ideas and memories of loss, then, will strike them with acute poignancy. Their daydreamy, inward reflections will make them seem apart from the family, and certainly very different from those days not so long ago when, at six or earlier, they were talking and engaging us in everything that crossed their minds.

Although this can seem difficult for us to absorb and assess, from very early on in their lives, kids catch a chilly glimmering of death. For many, the news will filter through by means of a fairy tale or a movie. For others, it will be the passing of a relative. (At around seven, for example, their cognitive powers, along with experiences in their own families and in those of their peers, permit them to calculate that older people are more likely to die.) For still others, it may well be the death of the family pet. And make no mistake: For children, as well as for many adults, the pet is an integral part of the family.

Of course, we want to protect our children from needless fears and tears, and that's a sound instinct to obey. But children already sense the truth that life is not permanent. While they cannot really come to terms with this fact of life (and who can, finally?), they need to know that their insight into reality is not misguided.

Grieving and healing from death is analogous in some ways to how we recover from a traumatic physical injury. If, for instance, a person has an open gash or cut, there are certain steps required to heal fully: applying topical medicines, washing the wound to prevent infection, reducing activity to allow the flesh to mend, changing bandages, and letting time pass. The same is true for the emotional wounds of loss and death, only now what is required is the space and encouragement to explore various feelings, to talk and express care for one another, to share memories of the person or pet who has passed away, to be silent together and apart, and to let time, lots of time, pass. We can even take the analogy further. If we have ever suffered a similar wound, the recollection of that earlier injury comes rushing back to us: We remember the pain, the recovery procedure, and the moment we felt healed. Emotionally, every loss we feel opens up onto other losses from our past. For Corinne, this may mean the earlier loss when her parents divorced.

While the death of a pet may or may not be of the same magnitude as the death of a person, the experience will jolt everybody in the family, and it will provide the occasion for many, many hard hours of talk, of silence, of mourning, of sadness. In the case of a pet, the grieving may not go on quite as long, but when we love our pets, we will be overwhelmed at first, and those first days in the aftermath are sure to be intense. A loss like that, too, may vividly bring up the recollection of other losses, encouraging us to revisit the deaths of people we have loved, such that we find ourselves grieving for much more than our pet. Grief is grief. Loss is loss. And yet grief and loss open profound doors into ourselves, into our past.

When Archie Dies . . .

Leanne would be wise to expect Corinne to ask questions about the details of the divorce, again. This may be direct. "Tell me again why you and Dad got divorced." Or it may be indirect. "How come I get dessert when I'm with you and Kenny but not when I'm at Dad's house?" In other words, Leanne needs to prepare herself.

For one thing, she should inform Corinne's dad about the state of Archie's health, as well as prepare Kenny for her daughter's onslaught of new questions about old events. Some of Corinne's old worries are going to show up again for tea, and with a little awareness, Leanne, Kenny, and her dad can help Corinne to keep it a brief and efficient tea party. They do this by taking the time to answer her seemingly off-the-wall questions about the past and by giving her the time and encouragement to connect the loss of Archie to the loss she experienced when her mom and dad divorced. And the way to do this is through being attentive to what Corinne is feeling and through exploring those feelings, not through overintellectualizing what she is enduring. Something along the lines of "You say you are sad. Does this sadness remind you of other sad times in your life?"

This is an opportunity for Corinne to revisit the split of her biological family from the secure perspective of the new life she has with her dad, her mom, and Kenny. And to the relief of everyone involved, Corinne will not need to travel too far or too long on this path for her to upgrade her understanding of that first loss and to make the connection to Archie as well. As a result, she will be stronger and more whole.

How We Deal with Death with Integrity

Integrity is about being true to oneself. Therefore, we need to give ourselves, and our children, the time and the opportunity to go through all the feelings and memories that are summoned up when death arrives: sadness, anger, sorrow, lethargy, fear. Or as Thomas Lewis, Fari Amini, and Richard Lannon write in their book *A General Theory of Love:* "Anyone who has grieved a death has known despair from the inside: the leaden inertia of the body, the global indifference to everything but the loss, the aversion to food, the urge to closet oneself away, the inability to sleep, the relentless grayness of the world."[2]

When we act with integrity in our grief, we begin by normalizing the strange and different ways everybody may be feeling: "It's normal for all of us to be sad and upset by Archie's death. In a way, this is how we show how much we loved him. After all, if we didn't love him, we wouldn't be sad. But our sad moods will pass in time. Kind of like that vacation drive last summer. Remember that drive? We thought we would never get there and we were all getting so bored and frustrated with one another, but finally we did get there and everything was fine again."

Archie's absence will be lamented for some time and in many ways. Archie's loss, for Corinne, compounds the wound visited upon her family. She may almost certainly find herself emotionally drifting, morose over the loss of the family that was her mother and father. Therefore, as she struggles to incorporate Archie's loss, she

may well feel unaccountably sad for her mom and dad, not to mention for herself, too. This is an altogether healthy and natural part
of grief, and the adults in her life can provide assistance by being
understanding of any shifts and swings in her temperament. They
can even go one better by naming, for Corinne, these same shifts
and swings in their temperaments: "When I saw some happy dog
walking the street today, I got very sad for a minute. Then I saw a
puppy running around, and it was weird, but I was really happy for
that little pooch. Archie was such a happy dog."

Death is a central, informing experience in our lives, and if we
believe that integrity matters anywhere, it should matter here.
Fundamentally, this means that we as parents affirm the sense of
loss we feel at the passing of a loved one. Important aspects of integrity come into play as we do so: commitment, strength, courage,
and compassion. Kenny and Leanne demonstrate their commitment to Archie and to each other and to Corinne in this hard
hour; they show strength by bearing up under the sadness and mutually supporting each other; they evidence courage by deciding at
great personal cost to reduce Archie's misery; they act with compassion when they take care of each other—and of Archie, too.
Corinne is noticing all this, and assessing the lessons.

In other words, we need to hang in with our kids in their confrontation with this messy and painful mystery. If kids think that
we don't find death to be anything other than traumatic, they will
have little basis upon which to examine their own complicated
and unresolvable feelings on the subject. We might think we need
to be stoic *for the kids*. But it's a fine line between a self-control that
denies the depth of one's pain and a self-control that suggests the
virtue of the struggle with the finality of death. Kenny indicates by
his grief that he has integrity, for it takes integrity and courage for
him to be so vulnerable and to do the right thing by Archie, even if
his heart is breaking. Often we hear people say they want to put
their problems behind them, and sometimes even well-intentioned
people suggest that mourning has some sort of time limit. But we

all grieve in our own way, and if we ever hope to be whole again, we cannot do so until we make peace in and with ourselves.

We help our children when we allow them to understand how loss is a fact of life and a terrible key to experience and growing up. We don't take away their pain by doing so; but by acknowledging to them that our lives and their lives will never be the same, we help strengthen them for the disappointments that await them. This is not being grim or fatalistic, either. Just the opposite. We model resilience in the face of loss, and this will give them a measure of confidence that while life can be chaotic, it is not meaningless. Furthermore, we honor those who have died with a respectful and authentic recognition of the place they held, and still hold, in our lives.

Integrity in Practice

For the above reasons, and because by its nature death is so cataclysmic and incomprehensible, children (and adults, too) may find a measure of consolation in ritual and ceremony. They will be fascinated by the biology of death, particularly physical decay, but they will also struggle with the spiritual, existential truths death opens up. Ceremony helps to bracket this type of seeking.

As a practical matter, in Corinne's case, she would almost certainly not benefit from being in attendance during the euthanasia procedure, but she will find a measure of meaningfulness and perhaps no small consolation in funereal rituals and remembrances of Archie. This will differ from home to home. Archie's life may be remembered through a tradition affiliated with the family's religious practice, for example, lighting a candle at church in honor of Archie. Or it may be a planned celebration at home with photographs, music, poems, food, and an immortalizing act related to Archie's favorite pastimes—the tennis ball that is bronzed, the collar that is hung next to the mantle, the leash that is forever left on the hallway hook. Or it may be an unplanned, spontaneous moment when pictures are pulled out of albums, when stories materialize from memory, and when tears of sadness and joy flow together.

The important part of any planned remembrance is that Corinne be invited to participate in the planning, and that begins with the simple question, "What do you imagine Archie would have liked?" Corinne will have answers to that question Leanne and Kenny never anticipated.

Leanne would also be wise to call Corinne's teacher at school to let her know about Archie's death. As a result, the teacher will be prepared and can, in her own way, facilitate Corinne's grieving and healing. This can happen by acknowledging Archie's loss to Corinne in a quiet one-on-one conversation, perhaps even relaying a similar loss in her own life. "Just a couple of years ago my sixteen-year-old cat died, so I know it hurts a lot." Down the road it might even mean inviting Corinne to bring in that bronzed tennis ball for class show-and-tell.

With time, Leanne, Kenny, and Corinne will begin to replace the emptiness brought on by Archie's death with the memories of his life. This celebration of his life, more than anything, is the best resolution any of us can aspire to in regard to his passing.

We have been talking about a pet, but the truth is that most school-age children will suffer the loss of a relative at some point, and the general course of grief and ritual is similar to what Corinne has been going through with Archie.

So, for instance, when a school-age child loses a loved one—parent, aunt, uncle, grandparent, family friend, neighbor—we should always ask them if they would like to attend the funeral. In other words, we need to give them a say. After all, they have had no say when it comes to death itself. That is why we should prepare them for the details of the funeral: open or closed casket, cremation, burial, reception. We also need to prepare them for the emotional atmosphere they can expect, such as grown-ups' crying. Children need information in order to make informed decisions. If your child wishes to attend, it is important that you make sure there is a trusted adult present who is also observing the child's behavior. That is, if this trusted person feels it is too charged an environment for your child, he or she can distract your child with a visit to the playroom upstairs or by suggesting that they go home early. It is also vital to give your child an out, some word or phrase that will let you know that the funeral is more than the child bargained for.

When Is the Right Time?

At some point, and probably sooner than either Kenny or Leanne care to imagine, Corinne is going to inquire into the possibility of getting another dog, probably a puppy this time, a dog that she can nurture from the start—a dog that needs *her*. Leanne and Kenny should talk about this eventuality before Corinne brings it up so that they can be prepared for a unified response. Practically, this means within the next few days.

Experience of time is much different for a seven-year-old than for an adult. For children, time is mostly about right now, which is why the present can be so intense for them and why their emotions are so fluid. Your son may go from tears at being rejected by a best friend to joy at his acceptance by a new best friend, all in the same five minutes on the playground. This means that if Leanne and Kenny are open to another dog, it will happen just before they think they are ready and long after Corinne thinks they are ready.

In a blended family like theirs, a puppy can become a beautiful symbol of the new home. This is an example of yet another new beginning to their family, and blended families cannot get enough of these beginnings with one another, as each one helps to absorb the losses from the breakup of the old.

four

Honesty

*How Can I Guide My Child
to Tell the Truth?*

"Why did you do all this for me?" he asked. "I don't deserve it.
I've never done anything for you."
"You have been my friend," replied Charlotte. "That in itself is a
tremendous thing. I wove my web for you because I liked you."

—E. B. White, *Charlotte's Web*

"WHO IS GEORGE WASHINGTON?"

It was Maggie's turn to pick up Ben. She parked her car in the
driveway and walked around the side of the house into the backyard. There she found Ben and his grandpa throwing the ball
back and forth.

Maggie and Andre were divorced and shared joint legal and
physical custody of their only child. Ben was about to turn seven,
and his parents had split up long ago, when he was a little over one
year old. To this day, and in their better moods, each would admit
that the other was probably a decent human being—just not the
right mate. It would be an exaggeration to say that their relationship was warm, but they were civil to each other and they had

grown more philosophical over time. At least they could manage a conversation when they met with teachers or discussed a visit to the pediatrician. Each was still living alone and each had a room for Ben. Arrangements and logistics could sometimes get pretty complicated, but their circumstances were fairly ordinary, in other words, no worse than all the other divorced families they knew.

They were in a way perhaps more fortunate than most, however, and that was because they could both count on Maggie's parents for child care. "Child care": That bland term didn't really capture the essence of Ben's connection with his grandparents. It was much richer and more involved than that. Fortunately, Maggie's parents still liked Andre, and he was a good father to Ben. In any case, Maggie's parents were both retired, and even in their mid-sixties they were both relatively vigorous and healthy. Grandpa had a cranky back that bothered him in rainy weather, and Grandma could probably exercise some more, and (as her daughter told her over and over) she should certainly give up cigarettes. She had cut down drastically over the years, when she used to smoke a pack or two a day, but Maggie was still hopeful that she would renounce the habit altogether.

Usually it was Grandpa who walked the two blocks over to school at the end of the day and walked home with Ben. That's where Grandma had snacks ready for him (and for Grandpa, too). Sometimes they would read together or watch television, sometimes they would play cards, or checkers, or go outside for some catch, like today.

"Mom, look! Grandpa got me a new baseball glove!"

Maggie came over and gave him a hug and admired the treasure. It was a beauty, just like the one her father had given her when she played Little League.

"You and Ben are quite the team, Dad."

"You know what they say about grandparents, Toots. We get to have all the fun, and then send them home when the mood sours."

"Then it looks like you two have a long way to go before Ben has to come in. I'm going to see how Mom's doing."

When Maggie came in through the screen door, her mom was busy, frantically searching through drawers and cupboards.

"I swear. I would lose my head if it wasn't attached."

"Let me help. What are you looking for, Mom?"

"Nothing."

"*Your cigarettes.*" Maggie had guessed right.

"I don't smoke when Ben's nearby, you know."

"Good for Ben. Just not good for you. Hope you don't find them."

"That's why I didn't ask for your help."

Maggie glanced at the kitchen table and the dining room and the couch in the living room, where Ben's toys and books and clothes were strewn. "Looks like Ben's having a better day than you."

"It's very strange," her mom mused. "That was almost a full pack."

"Oh, well. It could be a sign from above to stop."

Her mom pulled open the cabinet beneath the sink and was set to throw out an empty milk carton when she stopped and peered down into the trash. She reached into the garbage can and fished out a pack of cigarettes. "Hey, look at this," she marveled. "How'd they get there?"

"Maybe there's a secret part of you that wants to quit. Are you still listening to those self-hypnosis tapes?"

"Your father's going to get a piece of my mind when he—"

At this moment, Ben and Grandpa came in through the back-door.

"Harry, what's the big idea, throwing out my cigarettes?"

He denied doing any such thing, and the two of them went back and forth for a minute.

"If you're not fibbing, this is very strange," she concluded.

In that instant, Ben's mom and grandparents fixed their eyes on him. Somehow they all suddenly knew.

Maggie addressed her son. "Ben, did you—"

"No! Did I what?"

"Did you throw out Grandma's cigarettes?"

"Noooooooooooooooooooo. I have to go to the bathroom." And he scrambled out of the room and up the stairs, leaving his sweatshirt and new glove strewn with all his other things in the living room.

While Ben was in the bathroom, the three conferred.

When he came back, Grandma put a glass of milk and some cookies on a plate in front of him on the kitchen table, which pleased him, because these were freshly baked oatmeal cookies, which were to Ben the perfect treat. Also, he thought it meant that everyone had forgotten about the cigarettes.

"Ben," said Maggie. "You know the story about George Washington?"

Ben looked mystified and a little bit confused as to why his mom was asking about some guy he had never heard of. "Who is George Washington?"

Maggie told the story about chopping down the cherry tree and "I cannot tell a lie." Then Maggie said that she wanted to ask him a question once again. And he nodded, giving her the green light. She asked him if he had thrown out the cigarettes.

"Noooooooooooooooooooo."

"You sure?"

Ben was struggling, and so his mom was relieved when he said, "You going to be mad at me?"

"Not if you tell the truth right now."

"I was hiding them from Grandma. So she wouldn't get sick, like you're worried about."

"You were hiding them in the garbage?"

"I don't want her to smoke anymore." Ben took a bite of the cookie and chewed morosely. "I'm sorry, Grandma."

"It's OK, honey," she said. "Grandma still loves you."

Then Maggie spoke up. "You feel better now?"

"Yeah. Am I in trouble?"

"I'm not sure yet."

"You always say Grandma shouldn't smoke. I was just helping."

"I understand that you were trying to help Grandma, but when we ask you something," said Maggie, "we need to count on you to tell the truth. No matter how hard it is and even if you might be in trouble. In fact, it's even more important to tell the truth when you are in trouble."

Maggie was not sure where else to go right now. There had to be more somehow—it was too big a moment. She knew there was something really crucial to say, but she just didn't know whether she should praise him for trying to do the right thing or criticize him for not telling the truth. What *would* the perfect mother do?

"It's not good to lie, Mom. I know. You always tell me that. I'm sorry."

Whew! she almost said out loud, giving thanks he had made that connection.

"But Mom," Ben added, "you also taught me it's not good to smoke, either. Right?"

Grandpa rubbed the back of Ben's head and spoke to the ceiling: "Out of the mouths of babes . . . "

Grandma picked up the pack of cigarettes, threw them away again, and took the whole bag outside to the garbage.

NOTES HOME

Ben's Experience

On the surface, this seems to be a story about lying and taking something that is not yours. But from Ben's point of view, it is much more complicated, and before we go any further, let's unpack all that happened to him and inside him.

From the outset, he knows that smoking is bad for his grandmother. So he sees the cigarettes, and in the black-and-white thinking of a seven-year-old, he tosses them out. Out of sight, out of mind. At this point, he has no inner conflict whatsoever; in fact, he probably feels pretty good about himself. He is, after all, to his way of thinking, helping his grandmother to quit smoking.

Then he observes the commotion that ensues. His grandmother is a bit frantic, his grandfather is being chastised unfairly, and his mother appears confused, even distraught. Next, all the adults turn to him and intuit perfectly what has happened. At this point, he sees for the first time that he may be in trouble, just as his mom begins to ask him some hard questions. In response to a direct question, which has caught him totally off guard, he lies. From Ben's perspective, he likely never intended to lie. He simply reacts. He goes from feeling noble to feeling uncomfortable and guilty, all in the blink of an eye. On some level, he lies to buy some time to figure out what has just happened.

He makes additional time for himself by going to the bathroom. This gives everybody a chance to gather their wits. That is, he gives everyone a much needed time-out. Once he comes back, his mother wisely turns her attention just to the side, but not away. She tells Ben the story of George Washington—probably the same story that her mother or father told her a long time ago. And gradually Ben begins to grasp that he did something he shouldn't have done. This is the first time he senses his integrity is under siege. This is an enormous moment for Ben—making the shift from thinking that he has acted nobly to realizing that he has upset his grandmother and lied to his mother.

This is fortunately when his mother makes it possible for him to forge a series of connections, between and among his intention, his deeds, and his lying. When he lies, he is out of integrity, because he is no longer whole or authentic. What a lesson for Ben: Lying is both a symptom and a sign of being out of integrity. True, he doesn't persist in the lie, which is a testament to his integrity and which would pose a whole other order of problem.

So, what is the bottom line? Ben did the wrong thing (throwing away something that he does not own) for the right reason (he loves his grandmother). Keeping the focus on integrity rather than on the cigarettes or the lying invites Ben into this complicated un-derstanding. In short, Maggie is artfully creating the context for Ben to grow up with integrity.

Second and Third Chances

There is no final exam for integrity. We get the same midterms over and over again, even when they are not the same. Yes, on his first attempt, Ben lied to his mom. But as parents, we can never lose sight of the big picture, which is why Maggie was smart to give Ben another opportunity to get it right. If we expect perfection, we will be disappointed. But if we expect the best our children can do in any given moment, they will rise to the occasion more often than not, and so will we.

Take Ben and Maggie as an example. Had Maggie stopped all conversation and laid down the law, Ben would have become a very confused and angry little boy: confused as to why everyone was upset with him for helping his grandmother to stop smoking and angry that he was being treated (from his viewpoint) so harshly. By extending the conversation, Maggie increased the chances of Ben's coming clean. She believed in her son. She believed in her relationship with her son. He came through on the second try, which is often more difficult to do than coming through on the first try. To tell the truth on the second try means that he trusts his mom enough to know that she will put more value on where he ends up than on counting his mistakes along the way.

Honesty Versus Integrity

Out of the fullness of himself, and with a love for his grandmother, and with confidence that he is doing something good, Ben throws out the cigarettes. On some level, he has a glimmering as to the complexity of his act, which is why, upon being confronted, he scrambles around for a while and denies responsibility and disappears into the bathroom. He does so in all likelihood because the question he has been asked (*Did you throw out the cigarettes?*) feels radically off the main point. To him, not quite seven years old, the main point is that he likely feels brave and strong and *good,* and that, most important, there is a commendable purpose behind his deed. What could be more important than helping his grandmother be healthy and live longer and bake oatmeal cookies for him?

It is essential that Ben's mother and grandparents grasp the moral tension here. It is not a matter of the end justifying the means, either, because that philosophical distinction, while worthy of lots of interesting discussion between and among adults and older children, does not formally come into play at his stage of development. There is nothing self-serving or deceptive or expedient about Ben's action—just the opposite. And this is why Ben's mother has to stress simultaneously the following, and why his grandparents must support her:

- Of course it is good to love your grandmother and to be concerned about her well-being.
- It is understandable that in the moment it made sense to you to take matters into your own hands.
- Your intentions are noble.
- You lied, however, when we asked you a direct question.
- We all need to count on your being completely candid when we ask for information.
- Next time, consider before you do something if you can tell the truth afterward, and if you cannot, consider talking about your concerns with us.

Emphasizing one point over another risks simplifying a child's experience. Ben, after all, did not tell a falsehood in order to skirt accountability. Lying merely bought him a few minutes before paying the piper. Instead, if we communicate all of these principles, all of these values, and indicate that these are not always easy matters to reconcile, we go a long way toward inspiring trust.

Lying

"I cannot tell a lie," uttered George Washington famously. Or maybe, more accurately, once confronted with evidence (there's the ax, that's a felled tree), he leaps upon the soul-cleansing opportunity of taking responsibility. One of the reasons, perhaps, that the story of the so-called father of this country has attained mythic status is that we hope it confirms our deeper sense of how kids grow as a by-product of testing adults. In a way, Ben's story demonstrates that he (or any child) can lie at first for what seems to him to be an indisputably excellent, compelling reason (he is confused and scared for having done what he thought was a good thing), only to tell the truth later on for an equivalently excellent, compelling reason (he wants to live up to his parents' and grandparents' ideals).

When children do lie, especially younger children, they are usually caught, thankfully. They test us continually to see whether or not we mean what we say about truth telling. *Honesty is the best policy. Oh, what a tangled web we weave. . . .* In that endeavor, they are not necessarily being manipulative, nor are they necessarily taking advantage of our good-naturedness. Therefore, if in your mind your child has never lied, chances are he or she is a terrific actor or that you are not looking closely enough. Testing us is a beautiful educational tool for both us and them. That is why if you have a child who has a fondness for occasionally distorting facts, you can take solace in your being in the company of all other parents as well as your having numerous opportunities to reinforce the virtue of honesty.

Maybe you want to insist that your children tell the truth, the whole truth, and nothing but the truth. Indubitably, this is a worthy objective. With real-life children, though, and as they grow older, you might have to settle for most of the truth most of the time. (Adolescents, for instance, learn to tell the truth and omit the essence of your questions all at the same time. That is, they only answer the exact questions you ask, no more, no less. *"So you're going to a graduation party at Sherri's and you will be the designated driver?" "Yes."* This in no way says that your son won't be drinking, as more than a few teenagers mistakenly believe it is OK for the designated driver to drink.)

There is a truthfulness continuum for kids, but that does not mean that they are intrinsically moral relativists. They sense that sometimes they do not really know the truth or, if they do, how to express it. Or, as in Ben's case, we are asking questions that do not address the heart of the issue. What's more, they can be concerned that telling the truth will get them in trouble, without further discussion. Children, who are eyewitnesses of adult behavior, monitor the ways in which your honesty is hardly absolute and observe how your truthfulness takes place along a continuum of its own. White lies and polite distortions often grease the wheels of our social and professional lives. It may mean nothing to you to decline a dinner invitation on dubious grounds, but if your children know as much, they may be temporarily confused. *Sometimes it's OK to lie*, they can reasonably conclude. But when and where and how and why— these are complicated matters for a younger child to negotiate. It is easy to imagine, for instance, how we can avoid telling the whole truth on moral grounds. Our best friend has been drinking more than moderately, and she gets up to drive home. We have already confiscated the keys, but when she asks us where they are, we shrug our shoulders and say we have no idea. We tell her instead that the guest room upstairs is unoccupied. More important than honesty here is our relationship with our friend, specifically our hope to keep her alive. It takes a great deal of integrity in an example like this to finesse the truth.

When we discover our children in a lie, we likely endure a difficult time. We can flail for a while, figuring out whom we should blame. Are our supposedly pure-hearted children solely to blame? Have we misled them? Have we not furnished a proper example? Have they been corrupted by others, or by that vague construct called "society"?

If they hold the mirror up to us by forcing us to come to terms with our sometimes less than totally scrupulous standards, that could serve as a useful corrective for us, a kind of wake-up call for us in the pursuit of our own integrity. If we sense in them a pattern of misrepresentation, at home and school and all the places in between, however, we have some serious work to do, starting with being explicit in our assumptions and appropriately exacting in the administration of consequences. (It may also mean that we need to take a harder look at our own behaviors and start instituting changes of our own: Kids are great teachers in this regard.) True, kids have a fluid conception of reality, and the magical and the real often seem to conflict as well as meld in their daily lives, but it is the very rare child who does not consciously know when he or she is telling a lie.

In the end, since we do not expect ourselves to tell the truth 100 percent of the time, we should not be surprised when our kids do not, either. This means we hang in there with them when they miss the first opportunity to tell the truth when the truth brings unwanted consequences. Forgiveness is the daily bread of every family.

When it comes to honesty, it is easy to get on your high horse and preach in absolutes. It is just as easy to take the low road and use the easy way out. Both these options seem beside the point. Parents are human beings. So are their children. We all need to do better, and ultimately that's what being human is all about. With any luck, we will be able to look each other in the eye and say we did our best. The one dynamic we all have going for us is that when we have children, nothing will inspire us more to do better as human beings. For our children, nothing will motivate them more strongly to do better than their love of us, their parents. Our virtuous behavior does not determine their virtuous behavior. Nor do our lapses doom our children to moral laxity.

Out of the Mouths of Babes . . .

All parents have experienced exquisite embarrassment upon hearing their little darlings blurt out in public their blunt version of the truth. Usually, it is a perfect stranger at the supermarket or a relative at the Sunday dinner table who is the beneficiary of a comment that chills the social air. Theirs is perhaps a comment about an article of clothing, or about how somebody smells or talks or eats or looks.

> —You shouldn't say that.
> —But he has no hair.
> —You still shouldn't say that.
> —But he *is* bald!

What do you do with that? For one thing, when it comes to the education of younger children, who are rapidly becoming conversant with a big wide world outside the home and who are interested in confirming their sense of expanding reality, finding out if what they think is true is no trivial matter. Does that lady in the restaurant really laugh like a hyena, does that man really have a head as big as a watermelon, and how would they know if they do not venture their views out loud?

At first, it may be difficult for many younger children to reconcile the competing demands of two clashing principles. One, we want our children to tell the truth. Two, we want our children not to afflict others. That is, they need to appreciate the delicacy of the social fabric, the value of privacy, and the importance of maintaining appropriate boundaries between people. Fortunately, over time, and only over time, and with the aid of our conversation and patience, children can usually grasp the complexities adequately enough so that we can take them into supermarkets and restaurants without trepidation—most of the time.

What happens when a child like Ben senses a much deeper internal conflict—between doing what he conceives to be the right thing and lying about doing it? For parents and children both, this is a dizzying moment. In real life, truth telling can be messy, and learning to value integrity means sometimes we don't necessarily—or at first, anyway—quite tell the truth. Enter Ben, the liar, as well as Ben, his grandmother's knight in shining armor.

Grandparents

When our own parents become closely involved in the day-to-day lives of our children, wonderful results often prevail. So wonderful that in our kinder moments, we are tempted to take pleasure in our folks' conceivably doing a better job with our kids—or at least having more fun doing it—than we recall when it came to us. It is commonplace to remark on the unconditional quality of love parents hold for their children. But when grandparents and grandchildren click, that love seems somehow qualitatively different: It seems *unconditionally* unconditional.

Grandparents provide generational continuity. They tell stories about their own lives, about where they grew up and how times have changed. They give their grandchildren an invaluable glimpse into their own parents. As children ponder the meaning of their lives and their place in the grand scheme of their family, grandparents furnish crucial clues as to who they are and where they come from. We might have heard the story about that first factory job a million times, but for our kids, it is a magical first. This is history come alive. Their own history. In this respect, grandparents are deeply invested in integrity formation. Grandparents are able to look into the future with their grandchildren, beyond everyday trials and tribulations. Grandparents can say with 100 percent sincerity, "Don't worry about those lousy grades in math.

You're a wonderful and creative kid. You'll do fine. And one day, who knows, math might turn out to be your best subject and you'll be a rocket scientist."

In the cases of divorced families, grandparents provide increased stability, support of every kind, new perspectives, and love. Children cannot get enough love, no matter how warm and caring their home life may be. At bottom, grandparents provide a different kind of love and acceptance than parents do. Most are not burdened with daily limits, consequences, and discipline. As a result, Grandma and/or Grandpa's home is a magical place where rules, while not exactly relaxed, feel that way. Here, dessert without dinner is actually possible. (Not that anybody tells Mom or Dad, which is the whole point.)

Single Parents

Single parents have enough guilt. Everybody seems to be taking potshots at them. Cultural critics lay at their doorstep blame for school shootings, pregnancies, and raves. It's time to lighten up. Being a single parent is exhausting. It's expensive. It's lonely. It's overwhelming. And it's still parenting, with all the related risks and opportunities. Single parents, just like married parents, can be good, or bad, or anywhere in between. And the same can be said about their children.

Divorce has, once again, a suddenly changing face. Not so long ago, divorce brought a social stigma that perennially marked children and their parents. Then came the 1960s and 1970s, and staying together "for the kids' sake" no longer made the transparent good sense it once did. It is not surprising, however, that a new consensus is emerging lately, and the new wisdom superficially bears more than a passing resemblance to the old. Who knows? The corrective may prove useful and spare many kids the pain of growing up in split families. Even so, more than a few married couples will still be splitting up when their relationships sour. But no one will ever be blasé about their offspring's psychological and emotional cost. Perhaps at a minimum, people will be more pragmatic when it comes to marriage, realizing that divorce is too expensive in every sense, and therefore make better choices in marriage.

We ourselves are personally unacquainted with anyone with children who ever took divorce casually or did not fervently wish matters had been otherwise. And as recent U.S. census figures show, we have an enormous number of single parents, including over 2 million single fathers. You would be the rarest of exceptions if you did not know a split family. What's more, it can be virtually guaranteed that your own children, whatever their family status, mingle every day with children of divorced families, and these kids may well be their best friends.

Let us assume that Andre and Maggie, Ben's parents, did all they could to save their marriage, and let us also assume that their decision was mutual (or became mutual over time) and proceeded from their own sense of integrity. Does this mean that they necessarily set a bad example for their child? Does it disable them from instilling integrity in him?

Divorced parents, whatever their flaws, misperceptions, or misjudgments, are still capable of living in integrity with their children. If, however, they remain mired in the nostalgia for a past that no longer is available or if they still linger in anger and resentment, they may obliquely contaminate their relationship with their own children. Divorced parents can still be in integrity—and can still foster integrity in their own children—as long as they remain authentic and compassionate to *both* their former spouses and their children. This is a very tall order for most divorced couples, to be sure. Parenting in and through and after divorce is surely more complicated than it was before the breakup, but it is still and ever parenting, and all the usual considerations apply. It is still collaborative, it is still intense, it is still rooted in negotiation and communication, it is still the toughest and most rewarding responsibility you will ever enjoy.

It is true, by and large, that children from divorced families grow up faster. Most learn to become diplomats, adapting to the shape of the negotiating table. And they often feel excessive responsibility to protect the home and the family and both parents.

Splitting attention, time, and loyalties—these can be roadblocks to integrity. In the immediate future, and really up to and including high school, the pressures can be—if we are not carefully managing and monitoring—enormous, almost all-consuming. That's why many children in this predicament later yearn when they are older to go away from home to college. That's one place where they hope to relax finally, maybe because they believe it is now possible to lead one coherent life.

One positive thing: Divorce gives you lots of opportunities to engage your children in matters of the heart. That does not qualify as a cloud's silver lining, certainly, but it is helpful to keep in mind that there are some problems you cannot spare your children. Divorce stands preeminent among them.

The Integrity Conversation

It may be risky to say as much, but honesty in and of itself is never adequate, and it is never an absolute good—not for our children, not for our mates, not for ourselves. We can easily imagine situations in which people can claim to be honest even though they are taking a morally bankrupt position or urging the advancement of a corrupt agenda. Extremists of any stripe do this habitually. They articulate wholeheartedly and without qualms their dubious claims (about race, or religion, or whatever). And there is no doubt that, according to their own lights, they are being honest. But they may not be telling the truth, and they may have no integrity whatsoever. We embody integrity only when we exhibit tolerance of others' views and compassion for their lives. This does not mean that all views are equally justifiable or that all human beings are innocent. Hardly. Integrity does not mean resting in the misguided pseudo-libertarian proposition that "It's your opinion." Instead, integrity means resisting the spurious claims made by those who hate and by those who are willfully ignorant or otherwise misinformed. If you hold as your ultimate goal getting along with anybody, after all, you will have a difficult time maintaining your integrity.

Literary critics have often contended that *The Adventures of Huckleberry Finn* is the classic American novel. Perhaps the crucial moment for Huck takes place when he lies to protect Jim from the slave bounty hunters. In that instance, he risks his life and breaks the law—in order to keep his integrity. As Samuel L. Clemens (Mark Twain) would later characterize Huck's dilemma, "[I]n a crucial moral emergency . . . a sound heart & deformed conscience come into collision & conscience suffers defeat."[1] It took a literary genius to dramatize forever what parents learn over and over again from their children: They are much better than they think they are.

CONVERSATION BETWEEN MOM AND SON:
BEDTIME FOR BEN

—Is that your new baseball glove under the pillow?

—Is it OK if I keep it here?

—Sure. That's a sweet glove. Better than the one Grandpa gave me when I was your age.

—Do you think Grandma will really quit?

—It would be good if she did.

—Did you ever smoke, Mom?

—Funny you ask. When I was a teenager, I stole her cigarettes one time.

—You didn't.

—I did. And it was awful. I smoked one cigarette after another until I threw up.

—Yuck.

—You said it. Never smoked since.

—I'm glad you and Dad don't smoke.

—How are you doing? You had a tough day.

—Sorry I lied.

—You told the truth in the end, and that's what counts. Next time you'll probably tell the truth the first time I ask.

—Is Grandma mad at me?

—Of course not. She loves you. You know, trying to help her quit was a nice thing to do, it's just that the way you did it wasn't so great.

—I was trying to do the right thing.

—It's hard to know what the right thing is. Something Grandpa once told me might be helpful for you, too. Whenever you think about doing something, just imagine if you can look me or your dad in the eye and say what you did. If you can't, it's probably not the best thing to do. That's why you can always talk to us.

—OK. You still got your glove? Maybe we can play catch.

—We just did. But if you mean with a baseball, sure. Now go to sleep.

five

The Fight

How Can the Promotion of Integrity Increase the Chances of My Child's Not Becoming a Bully — or Not Being Bullied?

As I walked back to the village he followed me, shouting fresh insults. When I walked, he taunted, I staggered like an old cow; my woolen cap was absurd beyond all belief; my backside was immense and wobbled when I walked; and more the same sort, for his invention was not lively. I said nothing, because I knew that this spited him more than any retort, and that every time he shouted at me he lost face. . . . Then the unforeseen took over.

—**Robertson Davies,** *Fifth Business*

MOM'S SURPRISE

—One—

Judy arrived home twenty minutes before the kids returned from school. She was a little bit late today because she couldn't get away from work with all the deadlines piling up around her. She did the breakfast dishes, threw in a load of laundry, tossed out the junk mail, and put aside the bills for later examination.

As she prepared snacks for her son and daughter—Lewis, age eight, third grade, and Tracey, ten, fifth grade—she thought about what to make for dinner. It was going to take lots of creativity, given the resources staring out at her from among the depleted refrigerator shelves. Mom's Surprise—that's what the family called it—as in, the food was a surprise and it was always a surprise that dinner got served at all on such nights. She would have gone shopping before coming home, but time was short.

Maybe she would succumb to her husband's fallback pizza-delivery position. The kids never failed to rally around the pizza, and the same could not be said, to tell the truth, when it came to Mom's Surprise.

"Oh, well," she reflected, "somebody's got to be in charge of nutritional requirements."

That was when the door slammed. Which meant that Lewis was first home. How many times would she ask him not to slam the door before he got the message? Pick your battles, she told herself. Isn't that what all the books say?

"Lewis, that you?" Of course the door slamming told her it was Lewis, but she always said it anyway.

No answer. Now, that was unusual. She heard him scampering up the stairs to his room, which was also unusual. His first stop was normally the kitchen for a snack and a hug. She had an uneasy feeling and chewed on a carrot stick. She hated carrot sticks, and, call it mother's intuition, she knew something was up with Lewis.

Tracey then flew in the door, crying out, "You see Lewis?"

"He's upstairs."

"What are you going to do about it?"

"What am I going to do about what?"

"About what happened."

"What happened now?"

"You blind?"

"Tracey, slow down and tell me what you're talking about. Did something happen with your brother?"

"You mean you don't know?"

"Stay here. I'll be right back. Eat something."

"Any peanut butter?"

"Second shelf, refrigerator, in the back." Judy was on her way.

"Chunky or smooth?"

"Wait here," she shouted back.

Judy proceeded upstairs rehearsing a few of the possibilities. She hadn't heard from Lewis's school, so he couldn't be in big trouble. Could he? He had been having a tough time lately, that was true. He had wet his bed a couple of times in the last month, and when she recalled that, she had a horrible premonition. She hoped he hadn't had an accident in school. The other kids would have been merciless. Her mind kept working, creating one humiliating scenario after another. Lewis did walk home past the high school. Had he gotten hassled by some bigger kids? He could be a know-it-all sometimes. And he had been frustrated lately by his teacher, Ms. Morrison, who made him cry the other day. According to Lewis, she had told him to be quiet and listen for a change to other kids talk in the class. Judy had asked him, "She actually said to you 'for a change'?" Lewis reconfirmed the information, and Judy was still waiting to use that filed-away piece of data when she got an opening at a teacher's conference. Lewis was a very big talker, good with words, and she liked that he could hold his own in an argument with a lot of adults.

His door was slightly ajar, and when she knocked lightly, it swung open.

His back was turned to her and he was lying on his bed, his head buried under a pillow. Judy didn't know whether to stay where she was in the doorway or go sit next to him on the bed.

"Lewis, want to talk?"

"Yeah, OK." And he moved over a few inches on the bed.

She walked across the room, stepping over his books and back-pack and toys, and sat on the bed next to him. That's when he lifted up the pillow and turned his head toward her. And that's when she noticed the tears—along with his swollen, bloodied lip.

"What happened to you!"

Lewis was silent.

"Let me take a look." She did a quick assessment. She could tell he didn't require emergency-room stitches and that none of his teeth were loose. At the same time, it was amazing. Her little baby had been punched in the mouth. Somebody had punched her eight-year-old boy in the mouth. "Who did this to you?"

Lewis said nothing.

"Lewis, I need to know, who did this to you?"

"Nobody."

"Lewis, I'm just going to sit here till—"

"Jeremy, all right? Jeremy did it."

"What are you talking about, Jeremy? How'd that happen? I thought you guys got along."

"Jeremy, that's a joke, no way. He's a big butthead. I hate him, he's mean."

"When did this happen? What did Ms. Morrison do? I can't be-lieve nobody called me."

"We were on our way home after school and he punched me."

"Just like that, he punched you?"

"He's mean, I told you. He just punched me. I don't know why. Go ask him if you want."

"I'm calling Jeremy's mom right now."

"No! Everybody'll think I'm a sissy, which I'm not, and he's a butthead."

Judy found herself feeling totally confused. She reminded herself that it is never good to act in the heat of the moment. And she was furious with everybody—Jeremy, the school, Jeremy's parents,

Lewis's teacher, everybody. Why would anybody pick on her little Lewis? What was going on in the world, in schools? Couldn't kids be safe anymore anywhere? She caught herself almost starting to cry, but she was too angry to give over emotionally right now. Maybe later, after she and her husband, Roger, talked, then she would make the call, or he would.

In the meantime, she put her nurse's cap on. She took Lewis to the bathroom, where there was plenty of light to take another, closer look. He was going to be OK. Ice was called for now and a little TLC. So they marched down to the family room, where she plopped down with him in front of the TV with an ice pack. Then she had another thought. So she went into the kitchen and came back with a bowl of chocolate ice cream, his favorite. Now Lewis leaned against her. He had always been an affectionate little boy, but she couldn't help but notice he was pretty clingy right now. Considering what somebody had just done to him, no wonder.

After a while he seemed calmer, and he was giggling over what was on TV, so Judy kissed him on the top of his head, squeezed his arm, and walked back into the kitchen. There Tracey was, polishing off her bowl of ice cream.

"You know the rules. No ice cream before dinner."

"Great. Lewis is a jerk and he gets ice cream?"

"Your brother's had a hard day and he deserves a little treat so you can start acting like his big sister. Just because somebody picks on him doesn't mean he is a jerk."

"You think he deserves a treat? He got what was coming to him."

"Tracey, what are you talking about? Nobody deserves to get punched."

"Mom, come on. What the heck did Lewis tell you anyway?"

From the distance, Lewis cried out over the television, "Mom, any more ice cream?"

Judy didn't reply. She had a sinking feeling she was about to hear something she didn't want to hear.

–Two–

Roger got a call on his cell phone from Judy and, following instructions, brought home the pizza. Judy didn't feel much like cooking tonight.

"Is he up in his room?" he asked as soon as he got home.

"He doesn't need reconstructive surgery."

"So you haven't talked to him since you heard from Tracey?"

"I told him to stay in his room and that we'd all talk later on."

"Where's Tracey?"

"She's over at the Jenkins's house, doing her homework with Lynne. I think she just wanted to get out of here."

"I don't blame her. Tell me again what she said."

Judy told him. According to Tracey, Lewis and Jeremy and a few other boys were walking home from school. Tracey and Lynne were a little bit down the street, but she said she heard a lot of yelling and jeering behind. She heard Lewis making fun of Jeremy, something about his glasses, something about being in the slow-reader group. Everybody was laughing, except for Jeremy.

"I can't believe his school still segregates kids like that, into reading groups," he said.

"Anyway," Judy said, "apparently the other guys egged Lewis on and he was pretty mean to Jeremy. And here I thought they were friends."

"It's a guy thing. Kids can be pretty cruel to each other. Just never figured your child would be one of them."

"Those aren't my genes speaking."

And then Jeremy was so humiliated that, according to Tracey, he snapped and turned around and punched Lewis in the mouth.

"Is that it? Did Lewis fight back?"

"Is that another guy thing? No, he didn't fight back because Tracey didn't give them a chance. She stepped in between them, yelled at them to stop, and told Lewis to get home, which he did.

But like I told you on the phone, he didn't say anything to me about provoking Jeremy."

"OK, I guess I should talk to him."

"Why only you? Shouldn't we both talk to him?"

"Well, you and he have already talked. Maybe he'll give me some additional information."

"What are you saying? A boy tells his dad the truth?"

"Judy, this isn't about you and me, it's about our son."

"I can't stand it that my son is the kind of kid who picks on other kids. Part of me is glad he got his clock cleaned. Part of me, well, you don't want to know what the other part of me wants to do."

They talked some more before finally deciding to talk with Lewis together, up in his room.

—Three—

Roger started the conversation. "How you feeling, Lewis?"

"I got a stomachache, Dad."

"Looks like you have a busted lip, too."

"Mom, you told him, didn't you? Jeremy, he hit me."

"Your dad and I did talk. Only problem is, seems like there's another side to this story."

"My stomach really hurts. I think I had too much ice cream."

"Lewis," his dad said, "let's get back to what happened after school. Is there anything you left out from what you told Mom?"

"Like what?"

"Like maybe," Judy said, "Jeremy had a reason to punch you?"

"I was only joking. Everyone thought it was funny."

"Except Jeremy, evidently," said Roger.

"I didn't mean to hurt his feelings."

"But you did," both parents said in unison.

"Well, he shouldn't have punched me."

"You're right," said Roger, "but you shouldn't have picked on him, either."

"Nobody likes a bully," said Judy.

"I'm no bully. I was just joking."

"OK, but your joking got carried away," said Judy.

"You guys tease all the time. You tease Tracey about painting her fingernails. You tease Grandpa about his driving. You tease me about how I eat spaghetti."

"What?" said Judy.

"You do. You always say I get more on me than in me."

"OK," Roger said. "Maybe we all need to be more careful with each other. We shouldn't be teasing you about your eating, you're right. We can talk more about this another time."

"Your dad's right and you're right, too, Lewis. But let's get back to Jeremy. You feel bad when we tease you. How do you think Jeremy felt when you teased him?"

"Bad. I'm sorry."

Judy and Roger were relieved to hear that, and Roger noticed something else. "You look like you feel pretty sad, too."

"So?"

"You were mean to Jeremy, so you should feel bad about yourself, at least for a little bit. You've been through a lot. It's not so easy sometimes, is it, getting along with other people."

"Uh-huh."

"You're going to feel pretty sad for a while," Judy added. "But you know, that's really OK."

"Why's it good to feel sad?"

"Because you let yourself down by teasing Jeremy and bullying him with your words," said Judy. "Besides, what you're feeling now will help you never bully again."

"Actually, there is something you can do," said Roger.

"Will it make me feel better?"

"Not right away, but it's going to help when you tell Jeremy that you're sorry for teasing him."

Lewis stared in stunned disbelief at his parents. "He punched me."

"You're apologizing for what you did, teasing him."

"He should apologize to me for punching me."

"Maybe he will—and I hope he does," said Roger, "but that's his problem if he doesn't. What you're doing is about making things right with yourself. That's more important than anything else."

He knew they wouldn't budge, but he couldn't help himself. "Do I have to?"

In unison again: "Yes."

"If you want," said Judy, "we'll both help you find the words."

NOTES HOME

Roger and Judy

Lewis's parents sense the enlarged significance of this incident, and they understand that they need to be clear, careful, and unified in their approach. One: They must communicate to Lewis that his behavior was wrong. *It doesn't matter what you think of Jeremy. It's always wrong to pick on people.* Two: They need to understand for themselves what is driving Lewis to such behavior. *Is he having trouble elsewhere in his life? Do we tease each other too much in our family?* Three: They need Lewis to demonstrate that he is struggling over the same question. *I don't know why I kept teasing him. I couldn't stop myself. I wish I hadn't done it.* Four: They need to exact a natural consequence for his behavior. (The fat lip will not in and of itself suffice. Grounding him till high school will not work, either. Apologizing to Jeremy, though, would be an appropriate response.) That's the best hope for Lewis: to comprehend that he has crossed a significant line with Jeremy and that he has disappointed his parents. What his parents need to do is to help him understand that he has also disappointed himself. *You're a wonderful kid. You're smart, you're funny, you have friends. You don't need to act like a bully, Lewis. You're better than that.*

Of course, realistically, all this is not going to be accomplished tonight, or in one or two conversations. There is simply too much to absorb. Above all, everybody needs to resist the hollow call to "put it all behind us." Nobody is ready for that move just yet, and too much is at stake. Instead, they need to remind themselves that up until a few hours ago, they had no inkling that their son was even remotely capable of acting like a bully. One of the constants in our lives as parents is that our children are continually changing, and not always in the ways we like.

To Call or Not to Call

Once Judy determines that Lewis is physically intact and relatively calm, she is free to consider calling Jeremy's parents to inform them of Jeremy's unprovoked (or so she initially believed) attack on her son. Or is she? What about Lewis's social needs? That is, if she calls without consulting him, she may inflict more damage on Lewis than Jeremy's fist to his lip.

Imagine that Lewis's first version of the incident were true—Jeremy had sucker punched him out of the blue. Now what? She would still be wise to wait and take her lead from Lewis. Most eight-year-olds would not want her to make the call for fear of the consequences they would face the next day at school, though this goes against the grain of those of us who desire quick and efficient resolution. From Lewis's point of view, of course, a call to Jeremy's mom is the beginning of the end for him; he can imagine his new nicknames, "The Rat," "The Crybaby." The trick here is for Judy to give Lewis room to express and attend to his social needs while doing what she would want Jeremy's parents to do if roles were reversed; she would hope that they would call her and give her the chance to parent her son.

In addition, were she to call immediately, she would make a mistake common to most parents: assuming that the first explanation is the full story. No matter how good and well-intentioned a child (or an adult) is, it is the norm that most of us will leave out some of the essential details, the self-incriminating ones. Therefore, it is always wise to give the story time and then come back to it after you have recovered from the initial shock. You will come back with questions about the glaring inconsistencies. *He really punched you for no reason at all?* And he will have time to learn what it feels like not to tell the truth to his mom; he has squandered his integrity and he needs to feel what that is like. In short, he needs to feel bad for a while. That is, Lewis feels uncomfortable because he is out of integrity with his mom and with himself. This is good. These anxious feelings help him to understand and appreciate the importance of integrity in his life.

The good news is that given a little time, most children will divulge the rest of the story without much more prodding. They tell the truth about what matters. Eventually. (This points up the prudence of not calling the other parents too soon. If Judy had immediately called Jeremy's mom, later she would not only be furious with Lewis for not coming clean with her but also embarrassed and ashamed for having falsely accused Jeremy.)

You would do well as parents to tell your children that under extreme circumstances—a slur hurled at a passerby, a CD shoplifted at the music store, a neighbor's cat tormented up into a tree, or a punch—you have a duty to call. That is your responsibility as an adult and as a parent. Then let your children know that you will not make the call right away. First, you want to speak with them some more to see if they forgot anything the first time around and to get some counsel on what to say to the other parents and when to say it. That is, you can wait until the morning to call, if need be. There is no life-and-death urgency.

This tact makes possible a win-win situation. You discipline and support your children in helping them to learn from their behavior, and you maintain your integrity as a responsible parent as well. After all, in Lewis's case, what his parents tell Jeremy's parents can be both creative and honest. That is, for example, perhaps an unidentified, reliable witness heard and saw what happened and reported it to them. And now they are passing the information on, along with their concerns for Jeremy's well-being. This communicates the facts as to the incident and preserves Lewis's social status—and dignity.

We cannot parent well (if at all) without essential information, especially through the relatively complicated and unsavory moments. In this case, how Jeremy's parents respond will either be an invitation for more discussion—perhaps even leading to a coordinated effort on the part of both families—or it will be the end of the story as his family closes the doors to deal with the incident privately. What is key is that you respect the wishes of the other family and not impose your needs on them. For instance, it is easy to imagine Lewis's parents' insisting that Lewis apologize to Jeremy for his behavior, either in person or through a note. That is well and good. But it is another matter to expect Jeremy to apologize to Lewis, or to count on his parents to insist that Jeremy do so. That is interfering in the affairs of another family—and, in a sense, bullying of another order.

What Is a Bully?

Lewis is experimenting with bullying behaviors. He doesn't use his fists, but his words do damage to his classmate, Jeremy. As with all bullying, the opponents are mismatched. Jeremy cannot compete with Lewis in a war of words, which explains why Lewis employs these weapons and also why Jeremy strikes back in the way that seems most effective to him, by punching.

Without a doubt, bullies can pose an all-consuming problem for a child or a family afflicted by them. Although there are many things to be said about bullies, from our vantage point it is clear that they conspicuously suffer from a crisis of integrity. There is a moral emptiness inside them. Each time they engage in acts of intimidation or humiliation, they are asserting their power. Doing so, they temporarily feel full and whole.

On one level, bullies assert power over other, weaker-seeming people because they do not respect their victims. On another, theirs is a perverted search for the integrity they lack. In this sense, the exercise of brute power becomes a substitute for achieving wholeness. If children feel integrated, whole, authentic, and real, they have no need to tear down others. Bullying is the ultimate quest for self-esteem through disparagement of somebody else.

At the same time, it is very difficult to respect others if you do not respect yourself. And it is also very difficult to respect yourself if you have not been respected. This explains why bullies do not materialize out of thin air. They feel the need to assert their power in realms where they feel otherwise invisible and impotent.

Schools and families are rightly alarmed when they detect a bully in their midst. The key to dealing successfully with bullies is by limiting their sway of influence through identifying and tapping their vulnerability—through, in other words, making clear that you see they are struggling with their self-respect. Of course, adults need to control the demeaning behaviors demonstrated by bullies, but they also need to direct attention to the real problem, which lies deep within the bully. The dots need to be connected for the bully, explicitly. Will such an approach instantly revise such insidious behavior? Not automatically, certainly. But until bullies realize that the real target is themselves, they are doomed to play out patterns of self-defeating, aggressive behaviors. The trick is to make bullies understand that making others feel bad is ultimately going to make *them* feel bad. This is a hard sell, admittedly, for some bullies, but it is the best we can do short of banishment, and it is the only course to follow if we hope to reclaim them.

Similarly, the key to assisting victims of bullies is by identifying and tapping their own strength. They have been singled out, cruelly and devastatingly, but they need to grasp that they will not be broken down, even by the cleverest and most ruthless of bullies, if they maintain their own personal integrity. Children are capable of grasping this subtle point and can confront a bully most effectively by refusing to let the bully tarnish their self-worth, by rising above the terms of shame and disparagement. Integrity is the one thing nobody else can take away from us, and if we feel whole and worthwhile (to ourselves and to others), we can protect ourselves against brutalizing onslaughts.

As a side note, and as a practical matter, it is a sound idea, when helping the victim of a bully, to introduce him or her to sources of internal strength, perhaps through martial arts lessons or self-defense workshops. (Good martial arts instructors always stress ways to avoid physical conflict through reliance upon inner confidence and personal integrity.) What is more, such activities mesh nicely with the action-oriented world of children, and also speak to their deepest requirements for security, safety, and self-esteem.

But Is Lewis a Bully?

Based upon what we learn in this story and upon the way Lewis responded to his parents, it is clear that he is not a bully, just an eight-year-old experimenting with bullying behavior. How do we know this? Lewis concedes to feeling bad about teasing Jeremy. This is not how a bully would respond. Bullies tend not to feel bad about their behavior; in fact, most feel good about it even as they create elaborate justifications for picking on others. *Hey, it's a tough world. Better he learn to take care of himself now rather than later.* So Lewis's feeling bad is a good sign to his parents that he is not a bully.

In Lewis's case, there is also the influence of peers, which is an important consideration. Eight-year-olds experience peer pressure, and, just like the rest of us, are apt to miss the external signs (Jeremy's mounting frustration) as well as the internal signs (that feeling of discomfort and anxiety inside) that they are taking a behavior like teasing too far. No doubt, the situation never would have escalated had it only been Lewis and Jeremy. Again, this is different from the way bullies behave. Because bullies tease and fight as a means to feel better about themselves, they prefer, but do not require, an audience.

Finally, because his behavior was such a surprise to his parents, bullying is probably not a pattern for Lewis. Had that not been so, Judy and Roger would not have been so shocked. Frightened about where this behavior might lead, yes, but shocked, no. Does this mean they overreacted to what happened? Absolutely not. By taking Lewis's actions seriously and by engaging him in uncomfortable but meaningful conversation, they have underscored the severity of his breach of conduct and in so doing diminished the chances of its occurring again down the road.

That Yucky Feeling Vital to Integrity

We can be pretty sure that Lewis was feeling bad about himself when he came home and, without even saying hello to his mom, rushed upstairs to his room. But when Judy discovered him in tears on the bed, what was Lewis crying about? Was it the fist he took to his upper lip? Probably not. Sure, it hurts to get punched, and it's frightening to see and feel the flow of blood. But even more galling for eight-year-old Lewis is that the blow leaves a mark that becomes a constant reminder to Lewis of his having been, in the mind of this eight-year-old, beaten up by Jeremy. In this way, the scar is partly emotional, too. Each time he looks at his lip in the mirror, or feels it as he eats, or touches it with his fingers, he is also reminded of being humiliated by Jeremy. There is, however, one dynamic that we are overlooking.

When Mom walks into the room, chances are that Lewis is as concerned and upset over his role in instigating the fight as he is over his inability to defend himself. His provocation of Jeremy is what he's trying to hide from his mom, more than the fat lip itself.

In this light, at least some of the tears are attributable to how he expects his mom to respond to the knowledge of his responsibility in the fracas. And much of his distress relates to his attempt to conceal his role from his mother.

Imagine if Lewis believed that his mom subscribed to his first version of the truth. Instead of feeling remorse for his actions and taking responsibility for what happened, Lewis would feel "relief" at pulling a fast one. Sure, he would feel bad for a while, but probably not longer than it takes to finish a second bowl of ice cream. Worse yet, he would feel little remorse for what he did and thus would be more likely to repeat the behavior again in the near future.

Judy missed that first moment with Lewis. But as with most parenting moments, the opportunity comes back around—as when Tracey caught her mom up on the rest of the story. Now she has the chance to talk with Lewis openly about his behavior and his half-truth. In the end, Lewis needs a consequence to his action—more than a fat lip—but he also needs, as part of his behavioral consequence, to feel yucky for not having come clean with his mom. It is through these feelings of having let her and himself down that he experiences what it is like to be out of integrity with his mom and with himself. And like it or not, this is an important avenue to learning about integrity—by being out of it.

Conflict and Gender

When it comes to understanding your child, stereotypes are not always reliable, but at the same time, they are starting places for discussion. So here's one to consider. At age eight, most girls are ahead of boys in terms of verbal and relationship skills. In fact, theorists like Carol Gilligan have long postulated that for females, development centers on interdependence and relationships, while for boys, development centers on autonomy and individual accomplishment. Keep this in mind when trying to understand why eight-year-old boys are prone to fisticuffs much more often than their female counterparts.

With his focus on accomplishment and independence (and a relative paucity of verbal defenses), a boy being teased feels boxed into a corner with only two options—put his tail between his legs and flee, or fight. Girls, on the other hand, are more likely to spar verbally with one another much longer before resorting to jabs and hooks. When they do bully each other, they do so through controlling and manipulating their relationships with one another. A female bully can devastate by banishing someone from the lunch table, or by excluding somebody else from the birthday party, or by mocking somebody's new shoes.

So when it comes to boys' interpersonal difficulties, unless you take the time to prepare your sons for these inevitable confrontations by suggesting options, you should expect a fight-or-flight response. In an ideal world, it is Dad, not Mom, leading this kind of conversation with a boy. Many contemporary authors (William Pollack; Michael Gurian; Dan Kindlon and Michael Thompson) have pointed out the paradoxical expectations imposed upon males. Pollack formally named this "The Gender Straightjacket," which means that boys are expected to act under the old-fashioned definition of men—be tough, hold back your vulnerable feelings, be powerful, and don't show signs of weakness—and to act simultaneously like the new version of men and be sensitive, empathetic, emotionally available, and, within limits, vulnerable. In other words, boys today are stuck between two worlds, burdened by an evolving definition of masculinity.

Let's turn our attention to Jeremy. In these changing times it is only natural that boys look to their dads—and/or all their father figures—for the lead. In our case, Jeremy will learn much about being a man not only by what his dad says but by how he says it, too. Imagine if he were to scold, yell, and punish Jeremy. This would only reinforce the stereotype of males as tough and as winners. In essence, Jeremy may even imagine he reads between the lines:

"Good job, son." Or imagine if Roger said nothing and put it all on Judy's shoulders. Now Jeremy knows the female viewpoint on his actions, but his dad's silence may sow the seeds of doubt. *It's a guy thing, how could Mom understand?* Or worse, he may interpret his dad's silence as tacit approval. *Way to go, son. You're a chip off the old block.*

What is especially tough for Jeremy's dad, and most contemporary fathers in similar circumstances, is that what his son needs is probably what he did not get from his own father. This is, again, how our children insist we become better people ourselves.

The Eight-Year-Old

Is Lewis engaged in typical eight-year-old behavior? No, or, really, not quite. At the same time, it is not unusual for an eight-year-old to experiment with bullying behaviors. It's useful, therefore, to keep in mind what is going on developmentally and socially for eight-year-olds like Lewis and Jeremy.[1]

Eight is an exuberant year. With a better sense of themselves, eight-year-olds are excited to explore the outside world—school, friends, friends' families, new activities. They talk a lot (certainly more than six- and seven-year-olds) and about whatever is on their mind at the time. If you want to know what an eight-year-old is thinking, simply be quiet and listen. Enjoy this access and openness. In a matter of a few years it will be, we assure you, very different.

With parents, eight-year-olds not only want approval and support but also want you to want the same things they do—deciding when to spend time together, what game to play, what picture to draw, what to make for dinner. (So do not be fooled by what looks like a huge leap in autonomy; they still need you and it is more than they can say.) In short, these girls and boys demand and need lots of your attention.

At this age, they are also picking up on your worldviews, opinions, and attitudes. They are mirrors that reflect the best and worst parts of us, and usually at exactly the wrong time—in line at the grocery store, coming out of the movie theater, in the car with your in-laws. This is also when they are tuning in to the dynamics of your relationship with your spouse. And when they discover hidden anxieties between the two of you, they will not ignore this insight, either. Some will question aloud. Some will get in trouble, as if to divert your attention. Some will worry themselves into physical illness. Some will issue what sound like testimonials and proclamations and demands.

Because eight-year-olds demand lots of attention, it is no surprise that their relationships with siblings are contentious, and this is true for siblings up to two or three years older or younger. In their eyes, they are competing for your attention. No matter how meticulous you are in paying equal attention to each child, your eight-year-old will always feel slighted. Jealousy and envy are a perpetual heartbeat away. And, of course, with all this is the eight-year-old's penchant for taking out frustrations from school, friends, and home on siblings, especially younger ones. (After reprimanding your eight-year-old, you are wise to go hang around your six-year-old until all is calm, not giving your eight-year-old the opportunity to take frustrations out on a younger sibling.)

This is a year when friendship takes on more meaning and energy than ever before. Eight-year-olds look for more in their friendships—more time, more loyalty, more fun. This is an age when differences are also drawn and highlighted. The popular kids are apt to test or put to use their status by teasing and making fun of less socially successful peers. This means teasing, mocking, and imitating, often reaching a crescendo when they are together in groups. That is, when your son is with his buddies, his teasing will be more cutting, more insulting, more exaggerated, and more humiliating than when he is on his own. (Say hello to the not-so-subtle subtleties of peer pressure.) And these lines of difference are accentuated by eight-year-olds' preference for friends—they are drawn like moths to a lamp to kindred spirits and companions.

CONVERSATION BACK AT JEREMY'S HOUSE

Lewis's parents called Jeremy's parents. Later that night, while Jeremy is working on his homework, his dad stops by his room.

—Hey, Jeremy. Can we talk for a few minutes?

—I guess.

—I heard you had a pretty interesting walk home from school today. Want to tell me about it?

—I can't believe Lewis tattled!

—I didn't hear it from Lewis. But his folks called, and your mom and I appreciated that they did. So I want to hear what you have to say before jumping to any conclusions.

—Lewis can be so mean. He was teasing me like crazy in front of a bunch of his friends. He called me a big stupid jerk. His friends were all laughing at me, too. But it was when he said I was so stupid that I didn't even know he was making fun of me that I hit him. Honest, I didn't want to hit him, it just happened.

—Jeremy, I'm sorry Lewis teased you—what he did wasn't right.

—Did you get mad at his dad?

—No, I didn't, and you know, I have to tell you, I think what you did was just as bad. Son, I hate to tell you this, there are lots of Lewises in this world, so you're going to have to learn how to deal with them without having to beat them up.

—Yeah, I know.

—Really? You see, that's what worries me—that you haven't figured out how to defend yourself with words against guys like this. There are ways, you know.

—Like what? "Sticks and stones will break my bones but words will never hurt me" is for sissies. I'm not a little kid.

—Well, what else could you say?

—I don't know!

—OK, let's take a minute to think about it. You could have told him to grow up. Or you could have told him to stop trying to impress his friends by making fun of you. Or you could have just looked him in the eye and calmly said, "You're not worth getting in trouble over." Or you could have just said nothing and walked away from him. That way you don't give him the pleasure of knowing he got under your skin.

—Maybe.

—Maybe yes or maybe no? Jeremy, do you feel bad about slugging Lewis?

—No, why should I? He started it.

—I'm sure he did, but I'm concerned about you. That you don't feel bad about hitting somebody. How do you think Lewis felt when you hit him?

—It hurt.

—OK, but how do you think he felt inside?

—Bad.

—And how did you feel when he was teasing you?

—Bad.

—So you both feel crummy about what happened.

—I guess so.

—That's progress. A minute ago you said you didn't want to hit him, it just happened. What was that about?

—I just felt like I was going to blow up inside.

—I know that feeling. I get that way, too, sometimes.

—Really?

—I get that feeling more often than I like.

—Ever have that feeling about—me?

—That's a great example. Truth is, sometimes you've made me pretty mad and maybe I did want to spank you once or twice.

—But you didn't hit me.

—And I never will.

—I'd feel pretty bad if you hit me.

—So would I. And I'm glad you feel that way, because here's what you need to do—besides, of course, apologizing to Lewis for hitting him.

—Why should I apologize? He's the one that started it.

—Jeremy. I only said you have to apologize for hitting him—that's never the right thing to do unless you have no alternative to defend yourself.

—OK, what else?

—Before you go to bed, you need to write down, for me, five more things you could have said or done with Lewis besides hit him.

—Dad!

—Jeremy.

—OK. Can I do it later though?

—Actually, I think it's better if you do it right now. I'll be in the living room reading when you're done.

Jeremy's father was a bit late for the altercation with Lewis, but just in time for the rest of Jeremy's life.

six

Illness in the Family

How Can Going Through a Family Crisis Bolster My Child's Integrity?

Dad is touching my shoulder. Come on, Francis, you have to take care of your little brothers.

—**Frank McCourt,** *Angela's Ashes*

SANDWICHES

"I told you, wart. I told you I didn't want any mustard!" Ryan was ten, and his voice was anything but calm. "You never listen!"

"*You're* a fat green wart. You like mustard, get over it." Jocelyn, his twin sister, was dismissive, which is how she got when Ryan was excitable. They were headed for confrontation, and they both knew it. To tell the truth, there was something about today—they almost seemed to be looking for a fight.

"Stop being so bossy! Just leave my sandwich alone and let me make it the way I like. You're not Mom, you know."

"Wart," she decreed, again. Then, perhaps harder than she intended, Jocelyn pushed Ryan's plate across the counter toward him. The plate hit the floor just as their dad, Nate, came around the corner with an armful of groceries from Saturday morning shopping.

"What's all the arguing about this time?" Then seeing the bread on the floor—mustard side down—he added his two cents to the commotion. "What's wrong with you two? You can't even be in the same room for two minutes without fighting. Are you guys trying to wear me out? All I feel like I do lately is yell at you to stop this or hurry up and do that. So what's the deal, have you hatched a plot to drive your old man crazy?"

As much as she hated it, that last remark made Jocelyn smile. But she refused to give in, and instead shook her head from side to side, and she blurted out: "Who? Us?"

"Yes, you two, unless of course you're aliens posing as the twins, Jocelyn and Ryan. Now that I think about it, that would explain a lot."

It was Ryan's turn. "Mom says we're just spirited children."

Nate thought to himself, *That's* one *word for the chaos they routinely cause.*

"I think," said Ryan, "she means Jocelyn's loud."

"I'm not loud! *You're* loud!" shouted Jocelyn.

Dad intervened: "Guys, enough already, please?"

Then Ryan surprised everybody, including himself: "Anyway, you should talk. There's nothing wrong with Jocelyn and me, it's you and Mom. What's wrong with *you two?*"

This question knocked Nate back onto his heels. "What do you mean? Nothing's wrong with your mother and me." As the words came out, he wondered whether this was technically a lie. It definitely wasn't the whole truth, but he wasn't sure if it was a lie, either. Was he now mincing words just as his teenage son Billy did? Billy had been tough on the family the last few years before heading off for college.

The twins, now united, went on the offensive. First, Ryan: "Something's wrong. Where's Mom now? It's eleven in the morning."

"Your mother's resting. She's been working hard around here, to take good care of you two, I might add."

But before he could get even more sanctimonious, Jocelyn jumped in. "Mom never sleeps late, but now all of a sudden she's always sleeping in. She wasn't even up when we left for school the last two days. Something's going on between you two."

"Yeah," said Ryan, "you guys are always whispering to each other, like you're keeping secrets from us. And you both look sad all the time."

Jocelyn couldn't hold back anymore. "You guys are getting divorced, aren't you? And you're going to make Ryan and me choose who to live with. I know it! This is what happened to Jenny last year. Why are you doing this to us?"

Suddenly, Ryan was in tears. His more sensible and direct sister had used the D-word.

Nate, feeling like he had taken a punch to the belly, found himself falling back onto the kitchen school. "OK, Jocelyn. OK, Ryan. I'm sorry you think that. Look at me, please. Your mom and I are not getting a divorce. We're more in love with each other than the day we got married." Then he opened his arms as the twins ran into his chest for their dad's warm, familiar embrace.

Finally the three of them broke the group bear hug. But Jocelyn would not be deterred. "But Dad, then what is it? It's been weird around here. What's going on?"

"Well, I'm not sure where to begin."

"It's Mom, isn't it?" Ryan said. "Something's wrong with her."

"You two are pretty amazing. Nothing gets by you."

Nate nodded toward the living room, where they all sat down, twins on the sofa, Dad in the easy chair. The other easy chair, where Anita sat during family meetings, was conspicuously vacant.

"OK, you guys, here's the deal. You are right. Something is going on. Your mother is not feeling well. She has breast cancer, and we just found out about it on Wednesday, which is why we haven't said anything to you yet. We wanted to figure out what we were going to do before we talked to you guys."

Ryan couldn't stop himself. "Is she going to die?"

"No, Ryan, she isn't going to die." For the second time that morning, Nate wondered if this was technically a lie. He had to believe it was not.

"Is that why she's sleeping so much?"

"In part. But I'll tell you what. Give me a couple of minutes to go get Mom and then we can all talk together. We were going to wait until Billy got home from college, later tonight."

"Billy's coming home?" said Jocelyn. "Tonight?" Ryan said. The twins spoke with a mix of glee over seeing their nineteen-year-old brother again—and of dread. They sensed that Billy's coming home from college carried serious implications—a lot more than Dad was letting on.

NOTES HOME

Integrity in Times of Crisis

No one is shocked when the diagnosis of a serious illness, or the emergence of a comparable crisis, throws even the most stable people and families off balance. And so it is with Nate and Anita after they have learned of her breast cancer. They are not quite themselves, understandably, and so—also understandably—they have perhaps forgotten for a second just how much, and how uncannily, their kids pick up on the domestic emotional atmosphere. Therefore, as much as they try to spare the children, even temporarily, they will finally come up short.

While cancer, along with many other potentially grave medical conditions, poses special problems, to be sure, other crises can wreak parallel havoc on the family, and for related reasons. Job loss, addiction, financial hardship, marital discord—most families at one point or another will probably experience something that will induce panic and anxiety, something that will threaten their stability, if not their continued existence. The Notes Home throughout this chapter for the most part concern illness and its connection to the family, but they also largely apply to the other sorts of catastrophes. In all of these crises, integrity—expressed through compassion, honesty, openness, loyalty, caring—isn't always a pretty sight, but it is the surest anchor we have in the turbulence. (See the Postscript to this chapter for the way world crises affect the integrity of children.)

When trouble hits home, some of us adults, to be sure, try to be stoic, try to exempt others from worrying about us. It is not that we are attempting to deceive, simply that we are trying to shield our loved ones from the suffering. Sometimes it can seem like a good idea to control the flow of information, but the problem is that human beings—even ten-year-old human beings, and maybe *especially* ten-year-old human beings—can sense any gaps in the narratives we hold out. Control over something, anything, however illusory, seems valuable when life itself seems to be spinning out of control.

And yet, certainly, there are circumstances under which "information" should be controlled, or restricted, or doled out on a need-to-know basis. The truth is, however, that our kids' need to know is powerful. This is something appreciated by all parents who have ever driven their ten-year-old for longer than fifteen minutes anywhere. Children register at what seems like the cellular level the mysteries and secrets and crises we wish we could protect them from. That is where their integrity and their intuition align, and for that, we should be thankful. We *should* be thankful, of course, though at first blush we may be anything but.

Why Integrity Isn't Always a Pretty Sight

Integrity is too important to ignore or to push aside in the name of not making a scene. In fact, our integrity often requires us to push beyond the boundaries of politeness.

Were Jocelyn and Ryan graceful in how they raised their anxieties with their dad? No. Could one expect something more or different from a couple of ten-year-olds? No again. They did the best

they could, which was more than good enough. They unconsciously needed to make a scene of some sort in order to introduce
what they were feeling. Specifically, they grasped that Mom and
Dad were not being open with them, and furthermore, that something was so amiss in their home that they needed their dad to help
them match up reality with what they were feeling. That this confrontation comes about as a result of an otherwise mundane conflict is unsurprising.

In fact, if there is anything we can count on from childhood
through adolescence, it is that hardly ever will "the big issues"
come up when we expect them to; they will always slip in unex-
pectedly, and this is why parents learn to be quick on their feet. We
all worry about having the big "sex talk," or "car talk," or "drugs-
and-drinking talk," but in reality those issues can just as naturally
surface sometime between the eggs' being scrambled and being
served up.

Up until the instant that Jocelyn blurted out her concerns about
her mother and father, she had probably not even articulated them
to herself. In the moment of tension and confrontation, what was
just beneath the surface came rushing out, and not solely for Jocelyn. Even though they probably never formally discussed it, Ryan
was feeling the same way.

In many ways, the children were confirming reality by the way
they questioned their dad. Their intuition told them that something was wrong. But nothing was being said. Therefore, they did
what most of us would do in similar circumstances: They looked for
an explanation based upon their experience. The best they could
hypothesize was that their parents were divorcing, which was a familiar enough catastrophe to them, as they had already vicariously
experienced this through a friend. Their thinking would go something like this: "Mom's behavior has changed in big ways during
the last few days. She seems sad and scared. Dad seems to be trying
to cover for her or for something else. He seems sad and scared,
too. They are talking behind our backs about something that seems

to be important. What could it be?" The strongest, most powerful example they have that might warrant this kind of secrecy and sadness is divorce, so that is the conclusion they jump to. The ironic aspect here is that when kids think about their parents divorcing, they tend to seek the cause within themselves. So in this case, when Ryan and Jocelyn make the connection to the imminence of divorce, they are likely causing themselves additional pain, which is exactly the opposite of what keeping the information from them was meant to do in the first place.

When Integrity Knocks

Nate assured his kids that there was no impending divorce, and if he were another sort of dad, he might well have stopped there. After all, he and his wife had agreed upon a plan: to brief the twins after dinner when Billy arrived home. But he did not stay that course. Instead, he realized that no matter how well-intentioned he may have been—no matter how sensible the design appeared in the abstract—intentions, designs, and plans only take us so far. The kids picked up on the prevalent emotions in the home, which was a clue to Nate that he must improvise.

Letting his children dictate the next step in the progression of sharing information, therefore, was the correct move Nate could make to benefit the entire family. Now the kids would have their intuition reinforced, only this time with fuller, freer understanding. This recognition allowed one and all once again to support each other against the crisis impinging on their mom. In short, their family became whole once again, or as we like to say, in integrity with each other and themselves.

Will this information about their mom's breast cancer assuage the twins' anxieties? Of course not. They will still be upset about their mother. But they will not be carrying the extra burden of pretending all was right when they knew otherwise, and they will be stronger, and more confident, for helping to tear down the veil of mystification in their home. Bad news is frightening, but no news can be insidious and destructive.

If the twins had been five, the parents' approach would be somewhat different. We as parents would spare them details, follow their lead, giving out as much as they could deal with. We might bring another adult presence into the house, perhaps a relative. At five, after all, they cannot be self-sufficient. They will still need help getting dressed in the morning. They will still have to talk about school and friends in the same way any five-year-old would, and they will require as much normality as can be summoned up for them.

Of course, if the twins were, say, fifteen, we would grant them more responsibility, invest in them greater expectations. In general, we would invite them into as much as they can handle. Maybe they would go to a doctor's appointment, if they wished to do so. Of course, they might be frightened and repulsed by the chemo's results and therefore not want to be with their mom. And they may even rage against the entire situation, bitter that life has changed so much and that they cannot have a "normal" adolescence.

At fifteen, they would fluctuate between being like a ten- *and* an eighteen-year-old. So we would count on seeing both sides of their development. We would also not be tempted to take it so personally when they act like that nonexistent, mythical creature—a typical teenager. In general, we would accentuate the positive. And we would count on regression and, in general, the ordinary signs of adolescence. Now, not only would they be dealing with the challenges of their own teenage development but also with their fears as to their mom and family.

Twice as Nice—Yet Tougher Than They Appear

Ten-year-olds can rise to such a dire occasion as the onset of a serious family illness; yet we have to be careful both not to infantilize them and at the same time not to expect too much of them. No matter how "mature" they seem, they are only ten. At the same time, illness forces kids to grow up fast. Just be sure they don't grow up too fast and, along the way, discard their childhood. Children who grow up so fast that they become excessively serious lose out on indispensable experiences of childhood.

What are realistic expectations for ten-year-olds? At ten, they can take on more chores, do the laundry, get along with their siblings, and be considerate of their parents. At the same time, we should not expect them to be elated over being left alone or expect them to be in charge of their nutrition or to maintain a balanced diet. They will continue to need time with their parents, to play with them, to talk with them, to hang out with them.

Even under crisis circumstances, ten-year-olds are parents' dreams. They love their families and treat their parents as if they are infallible. Often they let others know the extent of your wisdom. "My mom says I can't stay home by myself yet, and she's right, I'm not ready." Home and family are the center of their universe. They enjoy time with the family and look forward to family outings and trips. You do a little planning and they fill up the space with good cheer and a positive attitude. In short, they are nice, and proud of it.

Boys especially get along well with their friends, usually other boys, when they are ten. Girls are a bit more complex, and their relationships with one another can run hot and cold. And sometimes their relationships with siblings can be trying. But with Mom and Dad, everything is sublime.

ICE CREAM

This episode takes place after Nate's wife has undergone a successful lumpectomy and is halfway through her sequential regimen of radiation and chemotherapy. She is done with the former and has just begun the latter.

It was close to midnight on a Friday evening. Billy and his dad were robotically spooning ice cream into their mouths, tuning in and out to what was happening on the television set droning in the background. They probably could not have passed a quiz that asked them to identify the flavor in their bowls or the show on TV. And they both had magazines on their laps, though neither was reading, more like skimming photos and article titles. More than anything, they were conversing in that intermittent, late-night style—too tired to go to bed, too awake to be silent. Still, there was tension under the surface, and something needed to be said.

"Nice of you to come home for the weekend, Billy. Your mom and I appreciate it. You're a big help around here, and Jocelyn and Ryan love having you around."

"I wanted to talk to you about that." He let the magazine fall closed. "It's hard being away at school with Mom going through all this. First the radiation, and now the chemotherapy. And the side effects of the chemo are much worse than for the radiation. You can already see that."

"It's been hard on her, but she's a real trooper. Never one complaint."

"You, too, Dad."

"What?"

"You're a real trooper, too. You're taking care of Mom, the twins, and still working fifty-plus hours at the firm."

"Keeps me busy, that's for sure. Though to tell the truth, I did speak to my partners at lunch today about the next couple of months. I simply can't keep putting in these killer hours."

"What'd they say?"

"Same thing they've been saying since your mom was diagnosed. *Take whatever time you need.*" Then he added, "It's just that now I finally see that I really need more and more time. Somehow, when the one you love gets cancer, you get a new perspective on your work. I've always loved doing architecture, but you know, times like this, it just becomes so damn clear how life is too short."

"That's what I want to talk to you about, too. Dad, let's face it, even if you cut back at the firm, you're going to need lots of help around the house."

"It's not too bad. The twins have been great. Just a couple more months is all."

"That's not true. Mom just started the chemotherapy. This is part two, after the radiation. She's going to get worse before she gets better. And it'll take time afterwards to recover."

"I just have to take it one day at a time. That's the only way I can manage. I was also thinking about hiring some help, for after school, a few hours a day."

"I've got a radical idea, Dad. I think I know the perfect person. Somebody you can absolutely trust, and somebody the twins'll even tolerate. Talking about me."

Nate was stunned speechless.

Billy continued, "I'm coming home to stay. For *now*, I mean, not forever, so don't worry."

"What are you talking about? You've got to get back to school to finish the semester. You've only got six, seven weeks left."

"Eight, but who's counting? But no, I don't have to go back. I already spoke with the dean, and she said it's not a problem. She gets that I want to be with my family. I'll have all summer to finish the Incompletes. It's all worked out."

"Billy, stay at school. We'll be fine." But Nate had already sensed the change in Billy. He seemed older, more grown up than he had ever noticed before. In fact, he sounded a lot like Nate right now, or at least how Nate imagined he would have sounded at that age had he been in similar circumstances. Besides, one look in Billy's face told him that Billy's mind was definitely made up.

"Too late, it's already settled. Just say yes, Dad. I can give Jocelyn and Ryan rides to school, to games, to friends' houses. I can help them with their homework and make sure they make their beds."

"Make their beds? What are you, the miracle worker?"

"I can do the shopping, too. Hell, I'm at least as good a cook as you."

"I thought you always liked my scrambled eggs and string beans."

"Nobody likes your scrambled eggs and string beans. But just stay with me on this one. I can do the laundry, too, and besides, I'll get to take care of Mom some at the same time. She's getting more and more fatigued and the nausea is getting worse."

"You would be a big help. You really sure about this?"

"I've never been more sure about anything. Plus, Mom needs me to remind her she looks fine with no hair. Maybe I'll shave my hair off as a sign of support. What do you think?"

"I think you've thought this all through, except that last part, about your hair." This brought a smile to both their faces. "You're really here to stay, aren't you?"

"Yeah, sure, for now. We need to be together. I need to be with you guys and the monster twins."

"You're probably right. Seems like you've been right about a lot of things lately. When did you go and grow up so fast?"

"Since I needed to. This is what family is about. At least that's what you and Mom always taught me. And I want to make sure Jocelyn and Ryan understand, too."

"Yeah, but I never thought you were listening. All through high school you barely looked at me—well, at least without rolling your eyes into the back of your head. I just never thought—"

"That was high school—everyone does that. Besides, I heard every word. I just needed to do things on my own. Just like you probably did."

"Wish you could have told me that a couple of years ago. That would have spared me a couple of these wrinkles on my face."

MORE NOTES HOME

Teenagers Grow Up Just out of View

If integrity is important to a child growing up, it remains vital during the mysterious and clouded time of adolescence. Part of the problem for teenagers' parents is learning how to see and hear integrity in new ways. In childhood, it is heartfelt conversations, honest interchange, consequences, support, forgiveness, and shared insights. In other words, it is a two-way street. During adolescence, it is much more of a one-way street: Parents remain focused on integrity in their dealings with their now angst-ridden teenagers only to have them go opaque on them. They seem to register none of their parents' profound insights or repeated offers for support.

But as we see with Billy, none of his parents' words have fallen on deaf ears. Quite the opposite: He has been paying attention all along. Only, as a teenager, he was enacting their lessons off to the side—perhaps with his friends on a Saturday evening, in his interchange with a difficult teacher, in how he treated the homeless during community service—just out of his parents' view. In his words, he needed to make his integrity personal. And to do this he needed to keep his parents from seeing too much. He had to do it on his own and in his own way, even if eventually it looks much like what his parents have been talking about all along.

Probably when Nate reflects on Billy in high school he will see anew many of the ways in which Billy was growing up—and growing up with integrity. He will recognize instances in which Billy had to learn the hard way, by being out of integrity. He will especially remember those moments when Billy was out of integrity in his relationship with his parents. Now, instead of remembering those instances as examples of his failure as a father, Nate will come to value those moments as being instrumental, ultimately, to the formation of Billy's integrity.

It Takes a Crisis

We tend to equate integrity with consistency. But sometimes being in integrity means we have to change our ways, often dramatically. It takes imagination and generosity to tolerate each other when we feel under pressure, along with a willingness to concede that though we may not understand what others are going through, we grant them the time and the opportunity to struggle in their individual ways.

In terms of these children, Nate and Anita will need to make special efforts to keep tuned in to their concerns. Nate and the twins have had the major conversation and cleared the air, perhaps, but that is only the beginning. Now Dad will need to reach out to their teachers and others in positions of authority, to keep them apprised of what is going on at home, and also to discover how well the twins are coping in school. That will give all of them the chance to be sensitive to the subtle (and the sometimes not-so-subtle) behavioral shifts that may take place. If the twins are especially energetic at home, they may become even more strident at school, or they may lapse into detachment. In either case, it is essential for both parents and teachers to keep themselves informed.

Regular check-ins with the children will prove indispensable, as well. Check-ins will also furnish opportunities for kids to ask questions and voice concerns that, it is guaranteed, have been eating away at them all day long. Check-ins may come in the form of scheduled family meetings. Being connected also means that you do everything you can to keep up routine, to keep being there alongside your kids. Kids need to retain their sense of hopefulness. And that hopefulness is contingent upon your valuing their daily existence. Involve them in your life and stay involved in the maddeningly mundane activities at home. The payoff will be that the mundane will become transcendent. Throwing the ball back and forth, sitting down to watch television together, shopping for groceries— any of these activities in the midst of a family crisis can be an occasion when you appreciate each other more than ever before.

Along the way, there will be failures, letdowns, and disappointments in any family constellation. We need to try to do our best, certainly, but we also need to be kind to ourselves when we do not rise to the occasion. When emotions run high, they can run erratically, too. Watching a loved one suffer and being helpless to do anything about it, we may lapse into behaviors we regret. And out of bickering and fighting with each other, the members of a family may sense a frustration they cannot relieve and a darkness they cannot illuminate. But here is the key: The futility and the discouragement we feel can be our signal to adapt. Within limits, give yourself and your children permission to be irrational, unreasonable, and contentious. At the hour when we are perhaps weakest and least capable, a crisis asks us to be more patient, more flexible, and more available than ever before.

In a crisis like this, integrity will always guide us. Acting with integrity means always being honest when our children ask a hard question and need to know the truth. Avoid false cheerfulness, and be careful to say exactly what you know without projecting any wishful thinking. Everything we say to our kids will be recalled, down to the syllable. And everything may not eventually be all right; breast cancer, while not necessarily the death sentence it once was, is a clever and intrepid adversary. We will ask our own questions, too, and not flinch when our children express their own anger and wishfulness. What's more, our integrity will also guide our children to the wellsprings of their own strength and integrity found deep within themselves. That is when the real surprise takes place: Our kids will give us the strength to give them the strength to endure.

When Parents and Kids Need Help

Sometimes we need to go outside the family for support in hard times. There are times when counseling—for ourselves, our kids, or the entire family—is the wise, appropriate response to the confusion and pain that crisis instigates. There is no cure for sadness, however. And there is no magic potion to erase the suffering we feel or see around us.

When your life is in utter disarray, however—when, for instance, sleeping and eating patterns are chaotic or when you are unable to function productively at work and at home—it is time to consider counseling for yourself.

When children are acting out at school, picking on each other or on other children, when they are not sleeping and eating adequately, when they seem morbidly preoccupied over the prospect of their own death—this is a time to consider counseling for them.

At the same time, sadness is unavoidable, and an absence of sadness is cause in itself for concern and attention. Yet no counselor can make us feel better about the suffering we or our loved ones are going through. But *feeling better* is not the purpose of counseling. Instead, its purpose is to put us *in touch with our deepest feelings* of insecurity and fear. If anything can help us when we are under duress, it is understanding that these feelings constitute our greatest sources of strength and that the courage it takes to face these fears and insecurities is exactly what we need to face the crisis that looms before us.

FAMILY MEAL: THE ANNIVERSARY

As they squeezed hands to indicate the end of thanksgiving, Nate raised his glass. "Let's toast Anita, your mom and my wife. It's been a year since your last chemo session, Anita, and we're here to give thanks for your continued health and to honor your strength and courage in all that you went through."

After the champagne glasses clinked, the twins did their best to follow the lead of their parents and brother. Each took the tiniest sip possible of their one ounce of champagne—though, to be honest, tiny sips were the only way they could make their celebratory drink last any longer than one gulp.

Anita took the spotlight. "And here's to my family for giving me the support I needed. Jocelyn and Ryan. Thanks for all the cards. Thanks for doing your homework without being asked. And thanks for learning how to do the laundry, and don't worry about that mixed load of whites and colors, everybody makes that mistake—once."

Jocelyn spoke up. "I told Billy not to do that, but did he listen? No."

"She's such a spirited child," Billy said.

"As for you, Billy," his mother said, "thanks for being not only smart enough but good and generous enough to realize that we needed you back home, despite what any of us thought at the time. Thanks for learning to cook and saving the twins from Dad's fast-food habits. And thanks for becoming the thoughtful and tender adult we thought you would become when you were a child. It's also nice to see that we both have some hair growing on our heads at last."

"Was Billy," said Ryan, "also a spirited child?"

"He was certainly a spirited teenager, Ryan, but don't you be getting any ideas, buster."

"I'm going to shave my own head when I'm in college," Ryan said, "just like you two."

"Now, Nate. Thanks, sweetheart, for taking the time away from work, then and still. It's great having you so much more present in our lives. Thanks for being courageous for me when you were terrified inside. And thanks for loving me so much."

"If we can please have your attention," Billy commenced. "Jocelyn, Ryan, and I have something we've made for you. And now's as good a time as any. Go on, you guys, go get it from the basement." In a flash the twins were jostling each other from side to side as they raced downstairs.

Billy just smiled back at his parents. "You know, they really are great kids, even if they are my brother and sister. Sometimes I can almost get why people have kids in the first place. Was I really like that at ten? What am I saying? God, they're eleven already."

When the twins came back into the dining room, they were carrying a big piece of poster board. When they set it on the table in front of their mom and dad, everyone could see the collage titled "How Mom Beat Cancer." In the center of the collage was a smil-ing and radiant photo of Anita taken just a week earlier. And ema-nating in all directions from that was a range of images and totemic objects from the past year: a small snapshot of Anita with no hair (and a smaller photo of Billy with no hair); a sweatsock dyed pink from having been washed with a red sweatshirt; a ticket stub from the baseball game last Thursday—a day game—to which Dad had taken the entire family; pictures of the twins' rooms—with their beds made; the URL for an on-line breast cancer support group that Ryan had found for his mom, which she had visited daily for the previous ten months; a note that Dad had written to the twins toward the end of radiation, letting them know that he regretted not spending more time with them; the title page from Jocelyn's science report on breast cancer; and a "Clean Bill of Health" that Billy had written and signed on the oncologist's stationery.

"I was wondering," said a beaming Anita, "what you guys were doing waving your new digital camera in front of my face."

"Billy showed us how," said Jocelyn.

"He's pretty handy to have around, isn't he? And all you guys are pretty darn good at keeping secrets."

"Yeah," said Nate, "but there was one thing none of us could keep secret even if we tried, and we didn't."

And they all knew exactly what that one thing was, and also that there was no reason to say its name out loud. It was all around them.

CONCLUDING NOTE HOME

The only constant in life, it's often been said, and wisely, is change. Sometimes, however, change can indeed wreak chaos in a family, and sometimes it can make a family stronger and, paradoxically, somehow more like it always was. In the case of this family, crisis eventually, gradually, painfully, brought out the best in each of

them. It would be presumptuous to think we can understand defin-
itively why this occurred, but one thing we notice throughout this
family's ordeal is the absolute commitment of its members to each
other. Everyone understood the strains each was undergoing and
everyone made generous allowance. They invested in each other
and trusted in each other.

Integrity and love are intertwined. We love out of the fullness of
our integrity, and we respect the integrity of others because we love
them. Certainly, love in the hard hours that illness brings to pass
can be tough to express and even tougher to take in. And yet, if we
all strive to be in integrity with ourselves and those we love, we
may find that it is just that love, which is so precious for being so
honest, that makes us free and whole and healthier than we
thought possible before.

POSTSCRIPT: SEPTEMBER 11, 2001

In a book about integrity, it is only fitting to reflect on how parents
can respond to an awesome national tragedy—because kids and
families may well feel dazed and distraught and anything but
whole.

In the aftermath of a tragedy such as the terrorist attacks in New
York City and Washington, D.C., or when facing the imminence of
war, we of course should pay close attention to our children's overt
and deflected responses. This means looking beneath the surface
and listening carefully for clues to their states of mind.

We could reasonably expect our children to be deeply affected,
and for a long, long time. At bottom, such a catastrophe is always
potentially personal for children—in much the same way it is personal for each and every one of us, even if we do not know a single
victim. We know that we are bound to all our fellow citizens of the
world, and our hearts are broken when we contemplate the devas-
tation visited upon the innocent. Our children register the seismic
shocks in the larger world and in the family, even if they do not

possess the sophistication to grasp them and even if they cannot articulate their concerns.

The closer we and our children are to ground zero, and the younger the child, the more challenging our response. But if any-thing is clear from this terrible moment, it is that we all feel close, potentially, to this ground zero, any ground zero. And those searing questions that will be asked by older children especially, about suf-fering and the nature of evil, will keep us close to them, for those are the questions that rightly burn within ourselves.

Deep, abiding feelings of fear and insecurity and helplessness may well persist for many children, who will not be able to abstract themselves or distance themselves, either. Keep the focus tight on them, for they are struggling to make sense, just as you are, but without your resources of experience.

As much as possible, keep in place family and social rituals and routines: These are profoundly meaningful and consoling to them when they feel the slippage of the underpinnings of their life. They see the newspapers, they watch the images that appear on televi-sion, they listen to their peers (or adults or older children) who are telling stories and giving opinions and spreading rumors. Monitor the news and television to the maximum extent that you can; the younger the child, the less equipped he or she will be to understand and assess; the older the child, the more interested he or she will be in discussing events and their meaning—and we should be ready to listen carefully to their views and their anxieties and their rage. Above all, be both realistic and supportive. Be the voice of reason. Be a beacon of understanding and sympathy. Be sure to convey your commitment to stand by them in their uncertainty. Let them know that even in a world in tumult, you are there for them in whatever way they need. Is that enough? Let us all hope so.

They might be wondering, depending upon their age, if they themselves will be killed. If their daddies and mommies will be go-ing to war. If evil people are going to attack them. Terrorists have many objectives, but among the most insidious is the design to destabilize the assumption that life goes on. Of course, we know in an awful way that this option may not be quite as available to us as it once was. In order to buttress children's sense of wholeness, we need to speak and act from our sense of wholeness.

Trauma. In the shock, ask questions. Listen to their questions. Be understanding of their fears, some of which may appear to be very irrational. Expect intermittent regressions in their behavior and do not overreact. A child who hasn't wet his bed in years may have accidents two nights in a row. Teddy bears may resume their once coveted standing in your children's lives. Your children will probably need more hugging and longer bedtime stories than before.

Normality. Don't vent in their vicinity. Restrain yourself from expressing your darker fears. Resume routines—games, dinner, conversation on other topics. Give them the sense of continuity. For younger kids, that means making home a safe and steady place. For older kids, it means that, too, but it also means giving them hope for the future.

Resilience. Their lives may feel suddenly upended, so we need to do what we must to give them the courage to act and to live in the seeming chaos. Your children are capable of bouncing back, yes, but they need the steadying ground of your presence to do so.

Response. Do whatever you can to help. Explain what you are doing to help—giving blood, donating money and goods. Children hate feeling helpless. Make it a point to involve them. Ask them to address the envelope to the Red Cross. Together, contribute to the community mural or memorial or fund for victims. Share a moment of silence before dinner.

Finally, the world may well have been geopolitically transformed by the events of September 11, 2001, but our children—of any age—will need to know that you and your family, along with the nation as a whole, while feeling great pain, are doing all that can be done to keep them safe. If we give children hope that life has meaning despite such catastrophe and that the future does not have to be bleak, we invest in them the most precious resource we have at our disposal: our rock-solid presence and our unconditional love.

seven

Tattletales, Truth Tellers, and Name-Callers

How Does Empathy Inspire Integrity?

I got most of my rebounds before you ever took your shot.

—**Bill Russell**

STICKS AND STONES . . .

—One—

It was Saturday morning and Gina's basketball team had a game. It was the nine- to ten-year-old girls' league, and in this conference the games normally fell into two types. One was something like 2-0 at the half, the other 56-2 at the final buzzer. The blowouts were always the predictable result of one team's having a ringer, the unstoppable kind of athlete who could dribble past everybody and score at will.

Gina's team, the Brown Bears, won a few and lost a few; it was in the middle of the pack. Not that any of the players could tell you with any confidence the team's win-loss record, because mainly they just liked playing the game and enjoyed being with each other. They practiced one night a week, for an hour, and they were always amazed when the one play they tried to run came close to working. The way it was *supposed* to work was this. "Bear Right" and "Bear Left" were just your basic pick and rolls. Though, to be honest, seldom did the pick and the roll occur on the same play, or even in the same game, for that matter. Gina was nine and a half, and she was the point guard, so it was her job to initiate the plays—left and right. She was a good floor leader.

Gina's little brother, Ty, was in the stands, along with their dad. Chase, her twelve-year-old brother, was also in the stands. In other words, it was family day at the local gym. Ty was seven and a half, and he liked, pretty much, watching his sister play. He liked it even better, though, when the two of them played at the park, because lately he was getting better, too. They were almost the same height, but she was much more athletic.

"Bear right," shouted Gina, as the play began to unfold, and then almost immediately to collapse, because her teammate had the ball stolen out of her hands and because her other teammate forgot to set the pick.

"Nice try!" her dad shouted.

To Ty, basketball was all right, but recently he had entered a very serious bug phase. Already he had a shelf of books on butterflies and beetles and bees, and he liked visiting natural-science web sites, and his favorite presents were DVDs on insect life. The Natural History Channel was the one he preferred watching.

At a time out, while his dad was across the way talking with another dad, Ty was listening to some older kids who were hanging around with Chase a few rows up at the top of the stands. Chase's team was there because the eleven- to twelve-year-old boys' league had the court next. Chase and his buddies were clowning around. They did that.

At one point, Ty heard Chase say to one of the guys, "Willie, where did you get that shirt? It makes you look like a fag."

Willie shrugged, noncommittally. "My aunt got it for me."

"Yeah, but you're the one wearing it. You trying to tell us something?" This made Chase's buddies laugh and give high fives all around.

Willie bit his lower lip. "Just leave it alone, Chase. It's just a damn shirt, is all."

"It's a fag shirt is what it is, and you must be a fag to wear it."

This was the cue for them to shove each other around, and everybody but Willie seemed to be having fun. Willie looked like he had a stomachache.

Then Chase and Ty locked eyes. Something had just happened that Ty didn't like, but he didn't know what or why he didn't.

–Two–

When everybody got home there was a funny mood in the air. Gina's team had won, and Chase's had lost. It was always easier when both teams won, and even, strangely, when both lost. Maybe it was that it was better when they were celebrating together or suffering together, because now it was hard to be one way when your sibling was the other. To Ty, sometimes bugs could be a whole lot easier to deal with than people.

Ty tracked down Gina, lazing in the sunny yard. "Gina, what's a fag?"

"I'm not sure, but I know it's a bad word and you should never use it."

"How do you know it's such a bad name?"

"Ms. Johnson, my teacher, once screamed at Tommy B. and yanked him off the playground and took him to the principal's office for using that word. And she never gets mad."

"But what does it mean?"

"Ty, did someone call you that?"

"No, I heard this older kid call someone a fag."

"Stop saying that word, Ty!"

"If I called you that name, Gina, would you get mad at me?"

"Yes."

"How come?"

"Because it's a bad word, and I'm not sure why. It's just mean. So stop asking."

"Would you tell Mom or Dad if I called you a fag?"

"I don't know. You know how they feel about tattling. I'm no tattletale. And neither are you. Come on, Ty, leave me alone. Don't you have some yellow jackets to catch or something?"

–Three–

Chase and Ty shared the same bedroom. Ty was studying the newest tunnel formations in his terrarium. He could watch his ants for hours on end.

Chase walked into the room. "What's up, bug boy?"

Ty started to tell him about the latest ant developments, but then he switched gears. "Good game, Chase."

"Thanks. You did notice we lost, right?"

"How come you don't like that shirt Willie was wearing?"

"What are you talking about?"

"Don't you like your friends? You called Willie a fag, and that's mean."

"I was just clowning with Willie. He can take it."

"But you called him a fag, and Gina says that's not a nice word."

"Gina, huh? Figures. It's just a word, no big deal. I didn't mean it, I said—I was just clowning, I told you."

"So he's not a fag?"

"How would I know?"

"Chase, what's a fag? What if Willie called you a fag?"

"He knows better."

"What if *I* called you a fag?"

Chase took horrified offense. "Drop it, all right?"

Ty turned his attention back to the terrarium, but he wasn't looking at the ants, he was just doing anything to look away from Chase. He felt relieved when Chase went to the bathroom and took a shower. Ty was very confused. Chase could call his friend Willie a fag and Chase would laugh, but if Ty called Chase a fag, his brother would be mad.

Ty still had no idea what the word meant, only that everybody told him it was a bad word. There were a few words like that, of course, words that you weren't ever supposed to say, because they weren't nice, but this word was somehow different. What's more, this was a word that everybody besides him sort of knew the meaning of, a word they weren't supposed to say, and yet it was a word they apparently all said.

He didn't know what to do. He felt bad and he didn't know why. Maybe he should talk to somebody. Mom or Dad? He couldn't decide. He was running a risk: Maybe if he even mentioned the word they'd get mad at him.

Just then Ty's dad passed by the open door of his room. "What's the news in ant world, big guy?"

Ty was happy for a question like that, and when his dad sat on the edge of the bed, he explained all he could about queens and soldiers and workers, but then he suddenly blurted out, "Dad, don't get mad at me."

His dad was silent for a minute, because he sensed Ty was about to announce a revelation. "Why would I get mad at you? Is there something you want to tell me?"

"I just have a question, OK?"

"OK."

"What's a fag?"

"Ty, where did you hear that word?"

"I can't tell you. That's tattling."

His father was waiting for more information.

"You and Mom always said don't tattle."

"That's right. You don't tattle to get your brother or sister or anybody else in trouble, because you have to learn how to take care of your own problems. Of course, if you can't handle something, it isn't tattling, and then you should tell us, so we can help you. So, that's not a nice word, Ty, and you shouldn't say it to anybody ever. Where'd you hear it?"

"The gym."

Dad waited for more and sat there silently.

Then Ty said, "It's not nice calling somebody fag; that's a bad name."

"Yes, Ty, you're right. You want to tell me who said the word? Was it you?"

"No!"

"So who?"

"You want me to tattle?"

"No, but I think you need to tell me something. Do you want to tell me something, Ty?"

"Do I have to?"

"That's something you and I are going to figure out. What do you say, you keep me company washing the car?"

"OK."

NOTES HOME

There are two enormous issues suggested by this story—name-calling and tattling, and these are subjects that are intricately intertwined whenever one or the other comes into play with our kids. Any time there is name-calling, there is someone registering pain or disappointment, which leads to tattling or to telling (or to silence). There is a season for each response, and we need to help our children negotiate the tricky passage between two very different options.

Words Will Never Hurt Me?

Every parent, everybody who can recall their own childhood for that matter, and even most Supreme Court justices know that

"Sticks and stones . . . " is absolutely wrong. Words can constitute a kind of action. Sometimes uttered words can heal, and sometimes they can hurt. And they can inflict scars that can be as lasting and uncomfortable as physical wounds. Furthermore, when mean-spirited words target others for their race, sex, disability, nationality, religion, or ethnicity, they harm not just the intended victim but those who overhear the remark, and even the people making such remarks. In short, harmful words or slurs are of another degree and complexity than your average, playground insults. "Jerk," "dumb," "stupid," while hurtful, are not nearly as indelible in their imprint. At the same time, don't minimize how damaging cutting remarks about how somebody looks or dresses, or where somebody lives, can be.

Of course, the entire issue of name-calling and bullying is now in the spotlight in a new and powerful way as a result of the possible connection between school-yard cruelties and school shootings. Many observers argue that school-yard aggression is normal and that most of us survived the onslaughts of childhood and adolescence; some think that we may even be evolutionarily hardwired to perpetrate such indignities upon others and that learning how to deal with such problems is an important learning experience for kids. Besides, they contend, you can't legislate virtuous thinking or enforce virtuous behavior.

Even if the connection between degrading speech and violence is never proven, however, and even if we are instinctively prone to such behavior (a proposition equally impossible to prove, of course), we still have an obligation to foster civility in our families and schools and communities. Perhaps there are adults who think that they themselves went through some manner of hazing or abuse at the hands of their peers during their school years and they like to think that they turned out all right. Maybe they did, or maybe they think that they did, or maybe they have forgotten the pain they felt, or inflicted, at the time. Nonetheless, if we require added incentive to do the right thing in order to make homes and schools safer places, all we need to realize is that the landscape has certainly changed in recent years. As we all know by now and to our horror, the means that kids these days have at their disposal to respond to taunts and brutalization are potentially lethal.

Not all kids are cruel to each other, but certainly many are. Some children, especially boys, may indeed go through their *Lord of the Flies* phase. Chances are high that at some point in their development, all our children can be counted on to explore a dark corner or two of themselves. Nevertheless, it is the obligation of every parent, family, teacher, school, and community to limit, if not eradicate, cruelty's sway, by both protecting and teaching the victimized and by both disciplining and rendering accountable the victimizer.

The term "fag," or "gay," used as an all-purpose put-down, like ethnic, racist, sexist slurs that need not be delineated, poisons the environment. Parents and teachers and everybody else should take such utterances seriously. Why Chase assaults his teammate and friend (and he may truly be a friend, too) resists easy analysis. It would take lots of conversation to unpack the sources of his attempt at "humor." What's certain is that there is anger somewhere and there is fear as well at the bottom of his comment. But it's not a joke, and it should never be tolerated as such. And once Chase has engaged in such behavior, his parents have the impetus they need to proceed with extensive conversation and education. The fear of homosexuality, and the anxiety as to one's own sexual orientation, colors this rhetorical gesture, just as the fear of "otherness" in general prompts other slurs. Sometimes it seems futile to resist such misbehaviors because we assume that our kids swim in a sea of abusive language and insult. Here's the good news. Many, if not most, kids do not like abusive language and insult any more than their parents do. The better news: Children can be taught (again, disciplined) to renounce such language and such crude and lazy thinking.

We all have an obligation to counter the culture of casual, incidental violence. We are not implying that every child who calls another kid a puerile name or who makes fun of what's inside somebody's lunch box is doomed to paint swastikas on synagogues or place burning crosses on lawns. But if we act with integrity and stand up to cruelty together (and teach why we do), we can help our children see that they are not only hurting other children but also hurting themselves, by undercutting their humanity, and their own integrity.

Boys and Name-Calling

The story in this chapter concerns a quintessential male version of name-calling: The slur that is tossed out in front of friends is intended to degrade the target while raising the status, in the eyes of the onlookers, of the victimizer. Words are hurled back and forth to the cheers and jeers of the crowd, and it all ends in a pushing match that leaves nobody the clear winner or loser. And the next time Chase and Willie see one another, they will probably act like nothing has happened, which is why Chase can pass off what he did as no big deal.

This is where adults need to intervene, to help both Chase and Willie see that it is, indeed, a big deal. The best means of doing this is through your reactions and your questions, the former stemming from your integrity and the latter out of a concern for your child's integrity. Chase can learn from others that it is wrong to name-call, but it is only through his own integrity that he has the freedom to declare for himself that it is wrong to use words such as "fag" and the like.

If you hear that your son has taunted another child, it is urgent to voice your anger, displeasure, disappointment, and sorrow. A parent should consider some sort of discipline—an apology to the other boy, perhaps even reaching out to his other friends to rectify the damage done to Willie. In all of this, however, be clear that you are mainly taking care of your own integrity, not your child's. Yes, he may learn through your reactions, but unless you explicitly tie what he has done to his own integrity, he is in danger of learning nothing other than to feel guilty. Here is the moment when a crucial shift in thinking can occur. When his father finds out (as we will see that he does), if he keeps Chase's integrity in focus, not only can he lead Chase to feeling bad about calling his friend a noxious name, he can nurture Chase's integrity as well. In this way, Chase comes to value his integrity enough to diminish the likelihood that he will ever engage in such behavior again.

Girls and Name-Calling

Girls name-call as much as boys, but in a slightly different manner. Girls are sneakier. That is, they use the power of relationships and groups not only to name-call but also to ostracize and destroy socially, especially at around twelve years old. Rather than hurl insults at one another, exchange some shoves and punches, and then move forward as if nothing has happened, girls form coalitions that eventually force the victim out of the group, often for good. Unknown to the intended victim, the leader of the group may have chosen her to be a sacrifice to the exercise of her own personal power. Over time she name-calls behind that girl's back to the other friends in the group. Then, in the stunning denouement the leader has been preparing for, all the other girls reject the victim as a friend—often through a note left on a locker or in a group e-mail. The result is that the victim is left friendless without having had a clue as to what was in store for her.

Unlike boys, who still eat lunch together and play on the playground with one another the day after an exchange of words and even a few fisticuffs, the ostracized girl is alone at lunch and at recess. Her spirit is temporarily broken.

Parents of a girl caught in such a dynamic—whether their child is the perpetrator, the victim, or the not-so-innocent bystander—

have to, like the parents of a son, intervene. For instance, if their daughter is the victim, they can confirm the horror and lead their daughter to be reflective about who her friends are and how to cope with disappointment. If their daughter is one of the bystanders, the parents can underscore the discomfort she repressed over watching somebody else being skewered. If their daughter is the ringleader, they can express their shock and affirm that, at least in their eyes, their daughter does not need to resort to such cruel depths and stratagems in order to be popular.

In all of the above examples, however, there is more work to do. That is, assume that a mom has spoken to her daughter, in each instance, from her own integrity. Now she must appeal to her daughter's integrity. This is never easy, but it's never impossible, either. Whatever role your daughter plays in these dynamics, there is a part of her that can empathize with others' positions. Empathy is a function of imagination, and imagination is our ultimate moral guide. It enables us to stand in each other's shoes, and it steers us toward our integrity. There is nothing truer about children than the power of their imaginations.

What's Wrong with Tattling?

When children tattle—or when adults, for that matter, tattle—they hand over to some presumed higher authority the responsibility they themselves *could* have and *should* have lived up to. Specifically, they act upon their less than noble motivations: They want to get somebody else in trouble, and they want to skirt the hard, lonely work of standing up for principle. When young children *tell*, however, they are taking responsibility by seeking the help they need in order to deal with a complicated and potentially hazardous situation. And these days, there's no more crucial distinction for our kids to learn to make.

So tattling is wrong but telling is right. Yet this can be a pretty complicated distinction for a child, even a smart, sensitive seven-

and-a-half-year-old like Ty, to grasp. Both boys and girls can feel the pressure to maintain silence or to rationalize brutality, especially when somebody is perceived to be doing something that *may* be wrong but something that does not on the surface seem to be hurting anybody else; or when somebody is doing something wrong that would not have happened if an adult were present. An emerging aspect of our parental integrity consists of this: When we explain what's wrong with *tattling*, we need to finish the job by saying what's right with *telling*.

Here's the whole real-world problem with the tattling-telling distinction. It depends upon the integrity of the person coming forward.

It may take a village to parent a child, but it takes personal integrity for a child to be a worthy citizen of a village. Only their integrity will steel children to respond to a genuine threat to themselves or others. It takes integrity to know that when, for instance, a friend stands in danger of harming himself or others, you break no honorable pact by speaking out. In fact, your integrity compels you to get help.

Integrity means standing up for yourselves and others. It also means knowing when you can't do it alone. Ty was in integrity throughout, which is why he kept voicing questions that nobody could answer. He stayed curious and trusted his intuition as he kept searching for answers. In this way, he was not only looking for the truth within himself, but he was also fostering honesty in everyone else.

Integrity Conversations with Chase

Complacency, Compliance, and *Cynicism* are the Three C's at war with integrity. As parents, we must be vigilant about disabusing ourselves of these tempting fallback positions when it comes to the behavior of our children. We abandon our children whenever we look at the world or at them through the lens of any one of the

Three C's. At heart, this is why raising a child can, in the long run, do much more for our personal development than any self-help book or guru. As we affirm our integrity in the name of our children, our kids teach us to be more genuine adults.

This education is a parent's payoff, and it is always indirect. Our integrity becomes stronger when we keep an eye out for how to connect integrity to the daily habits and views of our children. This is not at all akin to living through the accomplishments of our children. In fact, it is the near opposite. When we focus on their integrity, we are able so see how their accomplishments and failures are just that—theirs. We are free to be more detached from their outcomes and to be more present to them as fellow human beings.

Another Look at Role Models

Ty's dad has to connect with Ty and Chase—and he probably should touch base with Gina, too, once he hears that Ty has tried to talk with her, and their mother as well.

Kids need knowledge. What they don't know can hurt them. In this case, Ty needs to know what the word so crudely relates to. Already, we can assume, he has gained a dim glimmering of meaning through osmosis—by being in an environment in which the word is bandied about. But the meaning is likely to be inaccurate or distorted, so clearer information will help. This does not mean that his dad need be graphic in his explanations. Ty will let him know how much he needs to know. This also does not mean that his dad "defend" homosexuality or homosexuals, nor that he should somehow "promote" homosexual experience. The dad can be broadminded on the subject, or he can be opposed on moral grounds—it makes no difference, fundamentally, to his parenting. The issue is not about sex or sexuality at all. It's about tolerance, a value we cannot live without in a democratic society—or in our own family, for that matter.

So here is the dad's chance to promote tolerance, including possibly his tolerance of behavior or orientation he himself may not savor or endorse. Will he be speaking explicitly about sexuality? To a seven- or eight-year-old, a little information in this area will go a long way. Ty does not need much in the way of detail. He does need to be freed from his confusion by his father's concerted effort to demystify the term. Ty wouldn't be helped were his dad to decree, "It's a bad word. Don't use it. Let's talk about something else." And notice that Ty's father is pretty artful. He does not bar the doors and insist that Ty spill the beans. He counts on the truth coming out naturally as they wash the car together, and because they trust each other, the truth does come out, as we will see.

The bigger questions on the table here for Ty are actually much more interesting and formative, and they include these: Why must people be so mean to each other? What is sexuality? Is it true that some people have intimate feelings for people of the same sex? (This idea may seem like no big deal to younger children, whose best friends are of the same sex.) How can we protect ourselves and each other, including members of our own family, from being ridiculed or otherwise hurt or scapegoated?

Beyond that, Ty's dad is going to be a real role model of tolerance, compassion, and love. He is going to applaud Ty's perceptiveness, sensitivity, uncomfortable truth-seeking, and loyalty. Ty doesn't *acquire* his integrity from his dad, but his dad's calm, supportive response is going to testify loud and clear to Ty's existing integrity. By not freaking out and by speaking from the heart, his dad is going to help Ty the next time a difficult situation comes around.

The problem with the way we often talk about role models is that we tend to assume that kids cannot have values, or virtues, unless somebody else has them first. A dishonest, corrupt politician, athlete, or pop star does not cause our kids to misbehave any more than a principled politician, athlete, or pop star causes our kids to be noble. We are all more complicated than that. In fact, moral lapses on the part of others could conceivably inspire children to be *better*. Even so, however, Ty's most powerful role model is his dad, who has a chance to connect his son's painful searching for truth with the love he feels for him. Now *that* is something Ty will never, ever forget. All this explains why, despite the dominant culture of celebrity, every survey of kids comes to the same conclusion: The number one role models for children are their parents. After all, celebrities are not in relationship with our children, and relationship is the essence of role modeling.

CONVERSATION BETWEEN CHASE AND HIS DAD

—Can I go watch a video at Kamal's house? Dave and John and Willie and everybody else are going to be there.

—You guys can come over here, if you want.

—Kamal's got the video already.

—OK. His parents are going to be home, right?

—Call them. Don't worry, Dad. You know his folks; they're your friends. They're probably more uptight than you and Mom put together.

—Uptight? That's a compliment?

—Uh-huh.

—I wish I understood why guys are so mean to each other. I mean, I was probably the same way, so don't get me wrong. Willie's going to be there tonight?

—Ty is such a worm. What did he tell you?

—Let's not talk about Ty yet. And he's not a worm. He loves and respects you. You're his big brother, and that's a big responsibility. The way I see it, if anybody let anybody down here, it's you, Chase. Let's talk about you and your friends.

—Dad, we're kids. We say stupid things. Things we don't really mean.

—Except when you do mean them.

—The word just means stupid.

—Chase, the word means a lot of things, but it does not mean stupid. What does the word mean to you?

—It's, you know, it's somebody who does it with other guys.

—Can girls be gay, too?

—I don't know. I guess.

—And because someone does "it" with other guys does that mean they are stupid or less capable or worse in any way than someone who does "it" with girls?

—You're making a big deal about this, Dad.

—No, I'm not. And what worries me most is that you're not taking any of this very seriously. Then again, maybe kids are hardwired to be mean. You think that's true?

—I'm not a computer.

—I know, which is why I haven't pulled the plug on you tonight. Let's talk about your friends. Fortunately, we could also be hardwired to have friends.

—Dad, remember your small-talk theory? That we're only going to talk for a few minutes. No big talks.

—You're right. But you know the old saying, there's an exception to every rule? Well, this is one of those exceptions.

—OK.

—Whatever we're hardwired for, I'll tell you a few things we have to learn. Being mean to people, hurting somebody's feelings—that's never going to cut it with me and your mom. We also have to learn about friendship, about who our real friends are. The ones who really look out for us and the ones we really look out for. That takes some experience. We also have to understand what the words we use mean and how they can hurt others. "Fag" is a powerful word, stronger than you can imagine. In the end, if you continue to use words like that, you'll hurt yourself more than anybody else. So be careful. And in the interim, I never want to hear you using words like that again. Understood?

—Understood.

—And while you're at Kamal's tonight, take a look over at Willie and imagine what it felt like for him to have you pick on him in front of the others this morning. Then imagine if one of your friends is gay, how do you think they feel about you right about now?

—Hadn't thought of it like that before.

—OK, finally we're getting somewhere. You and your friends have a good time tonight.

—You are pretty mad at me, aren't you?

—Yes, but more than mad, I'm worried.

—I'll think about what you said, Dad. Honest.

—Good. And when you do, it should make you feel a little dissatisfied with yourself. One more thing. I hope the only thing you tell Ty is that you're glad he told me. If he didn't, you wouldn't have had the chance to never give him cause to tell me something like that again. We clear about that?

—You're right, I guess.

—I want you to have a good time tonight and, for no reason at all, just be kind to somebody. I have an idea. Why don't you start by apologizing to Willie? Words can heal, too, you know?

eight

Cheating

*How Can Homework Either Support
or Compromise My Child's Integrity?*

Oh, parents, confess
To your little ones the night is a long way off
And your taste for the mundane grows. . . .
Say there will always be cooking and cleaning to do,
That one thing leads to another, which leads to another.

—**Mark Strand, "The Continuous Life"**

READING THE KIDS

–One–

It was early evening in the middle of the week, and Bob asked his wife where Zoe, their daughter, was. Marsha was lying in bed, reading a novel.

"In her room," said Marsha, "doing what I'm trying to do, reading."

"You think it's good for her, how she stays shut off in her room reading?"

"Interesting. You want to make a case against reading books? Besides, she occasionally comes out to eat or go to school."

"You're right. I'm being stupid. Though I heard something some-where about eyestrain in kids as young as eleven, which she is, be-cause of reading too much, especially computer monitors. Oh, I re-member now. I read about it on my computer monitor."

But if their only problem with Zoe was that she liked to camp out reading in her room—well, they figured that was one problem they could live with. And so far, every eye checkup had been un-eventful for her—she didn't even wear glasses. In addition, Zoe seemed to love school, and she earned good to excellent grades in every subject. She even remarked one time that she liked her teachers to be tough on her.

"I can't remember working so hard," said Marsha, "when I was eleven and in the sixth grade. Can you?"

Bob could, actually, because he had been a driven student and remained ambitious to this day. "OK, that's one of our kids ac-counted for. So where's Pete?" Pete, who was nine, was unlike his sister when it came to school.

"Let's see, he was outside shooting hoops before dinner. It's after dinner, so he's probably watching basketball on TV . . ."

"That means he's not doing his homework. And what's new about that? Nothing. And what are we going to do about it?"

Marsha reminded her husband that Pete was in the fourth grade. Still, she conceded that it was curious how siblings can be so differ-ent from each other. Then they talked for a while about how it used to be, when they spent hours playing games after dinner, hanging out together, all four of them, occasionally watching TV when something good was on. Family Time, they once used to call it, sometimes even Quality Time, but that was a term that began to sound strange. Family Time. Quality Time. Now they just wanted *time* with their kids.

The kids' growing up was changing the face of their home life, that and all the demands the school made on the kids. And their lives as parents were changing, too. They came home later, they woke up earlier, they had more and more responsibilities at work.

Bob thought hard about all that for a second, and then he marched across the house and into the TV room, resolving, nonetheless, to take the bull by the horns. But as soon as he walked in there, he saw Pete enjoying watching the game so much that something made him hesitate.

"Who's playing?" Bob asked, even though he could tell exactly who.

Pete was riveted wide-eyed to the screen, holding a basketball on his lap, his high-top tennis shoes perched on the coffee table. Bob had the thought that Pete seemed to get new—and bigger— tennis shoes it seemed like about every three weeks. Was he already a size seven? Maybe he was an eight.

It was an important game between two college teams. "Five minutes to go, tie score. Sit down, Dad."

Bob hesitated.

"C'mon, Dad, sit down."

Bob sat down, and together they watched the teams really going at it. Bob could tell immediately that this was a terrific game. One brilliant play after another, the crowd was going crazy, the announcers' voices rising to a fever pitch. Father and son caught themselves rooting for the same team.

"Someday I want to go to that college," Pete suddenly volunteered. It was the first time Bob had ever heard Pete say something like that. He didn't know nine-year-olds ever thought about going to college, and he wondered what they thought college was about. Was it for them simply a place where cool basketball games were played and televised?

Maybe this was his opening to talk about school. At the commercial, while Pete kept his eyes fixed to the screen, his dad asked him how school had been today.

He received the usual abbreviated answer ("Same's always, kind of fun, sometimes"). But this time he added something. "Dad, can you help me with my math tonight? It's pretty hard." He said this in a very flat tone of voice that was tough to evaluate.

"Did you ask your teacher questions about things you didn't understand? You have to do that in school, Pete, that's the way it works, and it's not too early to start." This felt all wrong to Bob, but he didn't know what else to say, or not say.

Pete was silent. After all, his dad sort of answered his own question.

Bob reached for the remote and pressed the mute button, which caused Pete to look over warily in his direction.

"Oh, that's why you're watching TV? Because you needed help with your math?" That sarcastic remark just slipped out, and Bob wished he could take it back, but he couldn't stop himself. Fourth grade was being tough on his son, that much was obvious. It was a quantum leap from third grade, the teacher said during Parents' Night. Kids were thinking differently now, more abstractly, and expectations were rising exponentially.

Pete understood that his dad wanted him to go do his homework. "Can I watch the rest of the game first?"

Bob looked at his watch and did the calculations. Unless the game went into overtime, he figured it would be over by seven, seven-fifteen. That seemed a little late to be starting homework. It also crossed his mind that his son should have started his homework when he came home from school.

"How come you didn't get to work when you got home?"

"I did."

"What about the math?"

"I did the reading, and that took a long time. I'm sorry I can't read like Zoe or anything. I tried the math, but it was too hard. And you weren't home yet to help me, and Mom's, you know. I mean, Mom's not real good in math, she says."

His dad didn't see how he could get around pointing out that he'd had plenty of time to shoot hoops in the backyard, however. Something made him stop, though. One sarcastic remark a night was bad enough. Besides, if a kid couldn't shoot hoops when he came home from school, that would be pretty sad, wouldn't it? Instead, he went in another direction.

"How much homework did you get for tonight?"

Pete told him in detail, and his dad listened carefully. It seemed like a lot.

"Really? That much?"

Pete uh-huhed and both of them were relieved when the game came back on. Bob turned the volume up, noted the time left, three minutes, and settled in to watch the rest of the game. Afterward, he resolved he would sit down with Pete and see if he could help him figure out a systematic approach to homework. That's what Pete needed: a little more structure. Come to think of it, everybody did.

—Two—

Marsha was going to check in on Zoe, to make sure she was still alive. She really just wanted to say hi and talk a bit before everybody turned in for the night. Something, however, made her halt when she reached the computer in the hallway outside the bedrooms. The screen saver was flying with basketballs, which was in the program Bob installed. They kept the family computer there, so that the kids could have access and at the same time not get hung up in that private computer-generated world, surfing the net and so on. They had a few more years till high school and before both of their children could have their own computers in their rooms, and they congratulated themselves on this sensible, temporary compromise.

Marsha checked her e-mail. She had one address at work, and another at home, so she hardly ever received any messages here, but every now and then something slipped through. As she logged on to the e-mail program, a message popped up, with the subject "HOMEWORK," and because Marsha was a little foggy and tired, she reflexively clicked it open. Instantly, she realized she had made a mistake and that it was not for her, but instead for Zoe, and she started to back out. But then she couldn't help reading. It was from Lizzy, whose name Marsha could only vaguely remember. And this is what the e-mail said:

> *Zo heres my paper that i just finished i attatched it so you can just open it*
> *when you want if you use it and turn it in tommorow for homework*
> *change the words*
> *ok love and kisses*
> *izzy*

Marsha reread the e-mail. "Zoe, would you come out here, please?"

After a minute, and after Marsha called out for her again, Zoe rustled in her room and eventually opened the door and ambled out of the darkness. She had the glazed look she normally had upon exiting her room.

"I wish," said Marsha, "you would put the rest of the lights on in your room, that you wouldn't just read by that one lamp. Aren't you cold, not wearing socks?"

"I'm fine, Mom. You called me out here to talk about the lights and my socks?"

"What have you been reading?"

Zoe told her the title with a sigh, but then added sweetly, "You want to borrow it?"

"Haven't you read that before?"

Zoe said yes, but only twice, and so what? It was good. She should borrow it.

Then Marsha asked her about the e-mail.

"You opened my e-mail?" She squinted at her mother as if she were very small print on the eye chart that she was having trouble deciphering.

"Don't get mad. It was an accident, but I'm glad I did."

"I can't believe you did that. You going to say you're sorry?"

"I'm sorry I opened it by mistake, but I'm glad I did. Come here. Look."

Zoe complied. She glanced at the screen and said, "So?"

"So? Is that what you just said to me? *So?* I'll tell you *so.* Why is somebody named Lizzy sending you her homework paper? Are you cheating? And why's she call herself "izzy"? That mean something I don't want to think about?"

"I never read those things she sends me. She just wants to be friends."

"Did you tell her you don't read them?"

"And hurt her feelings? She's a little needy, Lizzy, and nobody really likes her much because—"

"Because why?"

"You need a reason not to like somebody? She just gets on people's nerves. Can I go back and read my book?"

"No. This is troubling. I want to get to the bottom of this."

"Mom, I'm just trying to help her fit in."

"This is not about Lizzy, it's about the homework she's sending you that you say you aren't using. Right?"

"OK."

"You're saying you're cheating, or you're saying you're not cheating? Which is it?"

"Mom, OK, sometimes I look at her stuff—"

"You just said you didn't."

"I'm no cheat, it's dumb to cheat. Sometimes I look at her stuff and sometimes I don't. Sometimes it's pretty good and I tell her so and she feels like she's helping me. But I don't need any help and I never use what she writes. My ideas are better anyway. Lizzy, she needs help, that's why she sends me her stuff. Look there, see? She even calls me Zo. You know I hate being called that."

"This is the strangest conversation we have ever had, Zoe."

"You call this a conversation? Feels like you're accusing me of something I didn't do."

"That's what I'm trying to figure out. Something's wrong here, but I can't put my finger on it."

Marsha looked at Zoe quizzically. On the one hand, she regretted having checked her e-mail, but on the other, she thought maybe there was something important to talk about—just as soon as she figured out what it was.

NOTES HOME

The Current Homework Debate

Homework is a hot topic once again. At the height of the Cold War—the 1950s and 1960s—Americans were concerned about Soviet advances, and there was widespread pressure to raise the level of performance expectations for American schoolchildren. Nowadays, however, at one end of the extreme, some educators and parents believe that schools routinely assign excessive amounts of work to be completed at home, contending it is work that could be performed better and more equitably at school. They maintain that insofar as individual family resources vary so widely, some kids are being treated in effect unfairly; that is, not all students enjoy equal access to computers, books, and the attention of educated parents. One way to level the playing field, then, is to restrict, if not eliminate, homework. Beyond that, too, these critics argue that by curtailing homework, we can actually strengthen family bonds by giving children more time to be with their parents and share in the life of the home. At a time when "values" seem to be slipping, they say, at a time when kids seem to be drifting away from the moorings of their families, isn't that an absolute essential?

At the same time, there are many other parents and educators who find those arguments lacking, if not specious. They say that one way to help develop the minds of our kids is by encouraging them to work hard and appropriately, specifically challenging them with reasonable assignments that complete or reinforce the work begun in the classroom. Not everything can be done at school. At home, students can enjoy educational experiences that are plainly unavailable in a classroom setting. There students can mull, and practice, and study at their own pace, building upon the lessons taught by their teachers. In their individual engagement with math or reading or vocabulary building or whatever else, they gain confidence and strength to return to school the next day to learn more.

Whatever your opinion, as we see it, there is good homework and not-so-good homework.

One way—perhaps the most efficient way—to know which kind your child is receiving is to find out from the teacher the rationale for homework assignments. The answers should make sense to you, and to your kids, too. Of course, we expect rising homework levels through grade school. At the same time, we want our children to enjoy their childhood and to have plenty of time to play and muse and be with their friends in unstructured environments. Which raises another issue for today's families. Sometimes, we may unintentionally overprogram our children. We should monitor whether or not they are being burdened by too many after-school and weekend activities. When they come home after classes, and practices, and games, do they have energy left to enjoy family dinner, for instance, and do they have the chance to be alone with themselves and their own thinking?

Homework is always going to be a part of a child's life. Yet every child (and adult) needs downtime after school (or after work). This means different things for different kids. For some, like Pete, it will mean going outside and shooting hoops. For some it will be watching a little television. For some it will mean hanging out with friends in the neighborhood. (And for some—including most, if not all, teenagers—it will mean being in their rooms with the door closed listening to loud music.) After downtime and homework are factored in, we as parents can focus on what, if anything, can be added to our children's schedules without tipping the balance.

When kids approach their homework with a seriousness of purpose, and when their lives have balance, good things happen intellectually and developmentally. Keep in mind, too, that by the time our children reach high school, and if they attend schools that foster the academic life, they will be having close to forty-five minutes of homework a night per subject. It behooves us, then, to help them prepare for those eventualities. Even so, we have a role to play by encouraging them to struggle with their academic difficulties as much as we celebrate their achievements in and out of school.

Parenting 101

While we strive to support our individual children's academic work fairly, we must sometimes treat them differently, according to their unique needs and requirements. In the case of this family, it means prodding Pete to do more and granting more independence to Zoe. After all, Pete has been engaging in avoidance and deferral strategies when it comes to doing his homework, so he will benefit from increased direction, until he is older and capable of doing this on his own.

As a consequence, Bob and Marsha might need to set a formal time for Pete to do his homework each night, which is a structure that Zoe does not and probably never will need. To Pete this may appear onerous or unfair. "How come Zoe doesn't have to do her homework right after dinner?" No two children are alike, and thus each needs to be treated differently. Because kids are so tuned in to issues of justice, they tend to miss this point, but parents cannot afford to do so.

In general, we help our kids with homework most effectively by not taking over their work, no matter how difficult it may be. That is a matter of our own integrity and of theirs, too. We stay engaged with them by acting with discipline. And we model discipline ourselves when we encourage our kids to learn for themselves. In other words, Pete's dad can underscore Pete's integrity in key ways: (1) He can make clear that it is appropriate to ask for help when you need it—an opportunity he initially missed while he was watching the game with Pete, who asked him for help; (2) he can encourage Pete to push himself to do his work; and (3) he can make clear the limits of his own involvement by making sure that Pete does his own work, even with the help he legitimately may need.

If Bob made one mistake on this particular night with Pete, it lay in his assumption that Pete knew how to reach out for help. *"Did you ask your teacher questions about things you didn't understand? You have to do that in school, Pete, that's the way it works, and it's not too early to start."* But many kids need to learn how to do that. So for children like Pete who have trouble asking teachers for help, parents can play the role of educator, by encouraging them to take a risk to reach out when in doubt. They can also work behind the scenes, reaching out themselves to teachers in order to fill them in on their children's struggles to ask questions: *"Pete has trouble asking for help when he gets confused. We talked tonight about how it's OK to be confused and it's OK to ask questions. And he said he's going to try tomorrow. So if you can just be on the lookout, maybe we can all help him develop a nice new habit."*

Yes, it is certainly painful to watch our kids struggling with a difficult assignment. Of course, if you think the assignment is too difficult, or inappropriately time-consuming, you have a conversation looming in the future, but it's one you should have with your child's teacher. At that point, with any luck, you may well have a chance to understand the intellectual rationale for the work and maybe appreciate better the life your children have in school. More than anything, these are the occasions when we need to stay in the moment with our kids and their struggles, even as we build a bridge toward the experiences that await them, when, in high school and beyond, they will feel increasingly tested and tried.

Putting the Home Back in Homework

Much is made of the importance of families having dinner together, and unquestionably, there is a lot of merit to the notion.

Something invaluable is lost when everybody is on a different schedule, when some eat standing at the kitchen counter, and when there is no chance simply to be with each other at the end of the workday and school day.

We can make the home academically friendly by turning off the television and computer, and by hanging out close enough—within striking or shouting distance of each other—as the kids do homework and we engage in our own quiet activities. If we can make a few hours sacrosanct in the home for quiet and contemplation and private work, we go a long way toward promoting independence and creativity in our kids. This also creates feelings of interdependency, when children can easily ask for assistance with their homework and when our quiet presence is the exact support our kids need to persevere through a tough problem or a less than thrilling assignment. This is the type of environment that promotes family.

This kind of environment will pay enormous dividends down the road, in high school, when, in our kids' minds, we move to the periphery. Despite what they might tell us, when our children become teenagers, they will still value our presence at home. We do not need to be in their rooms or hovering over their desks to provide support as long as they can feel our presence—even when we are not next to them.

Nine- and Eleven-Year-Olds: Alone Together

Pete is a typical nine-year-old. Like most kids his age, he is defensive about his weaknesses. He wants to do what he wants to do when he wants to do it. He is inconsistent, and barely notices, because all of his life is of a piece. It is a small step from shooting hoops to doing his homework to watching a game to talking with Dad to going to college. Nine-year-olds have an active fantasy life. But they do not distinguish easily between fantasy and reality.

Zoe is not a typical eleven-year-old. Most eleven-year-olds like to be the center of the family action. They don't like to spend time alone in their rooms. They do their homework on the dining-room table, so as to not miss anything going on. At the same time, an introverted child like Zoe would find her room a perfect hideout from her attention-seeking brother pounding his basketball in the hallway. Fortunately, this sibling split is probably only a phase; it wasn't long ago that they played together, and it won't be too far in the future before they are comparing notes about Mom and Dad. But like most eleven-year-olds, Zoe is sharp and perceptive and does not take as gospel truth everything her parents say.

Nine-year-olds are famous for getting along with their siblings, while eleven-year-olds are not. Nine-year-olds look up to their older siblings, and eleven-year-olds wish they were only children. So what happens in such a family constellation? Pestering. Teasing. Competition. Missing CDs. Thousand-yard stares exchanged between the two of them. Parents' exhaustion: interventions, separations, defenses, pleadings.

Cheating and Integrity

Sometimes it takes a call from a teacher for parents to engage in the cheating-and-integrity conversation with their children. That is when we get the news that ruins our day about how our child has resorted to unethical behavior. These things do indeed happen. As we discuss in the next section, even good kids from good families may experiment with cheating.

Although it will be tough to maintain our equanimity when we get that fateful call, we must strive to do exactly that. One thing we should keep in mind is that we should be thankful the school is taking the matter seriously. The other thing to keep in mind is that it is actually a good thing that our child was caught. Now, we have an opportunity to face this problem directly.

If ever you have the golden opportunity to underscore the meaning of integrity, cheating is the one. There are many reasons to cheat. There is ultimately only one reason not to cheat: integrity. You want your children to understand that the "rewards" of cheating are poisonous. Yes, they may indeed get the higher grade or skate by, but only at the cost of damaging themselves through misrepresentation of themselves and their work, and this is a price that they cannot pay and at the same time remain content with themselves.

Your children will feel distraught and unsettled by being caught cheating. This is good. What is essential to get across, though, is that nobody else is making them feel this way. They are doing it to themselves. That is, instead of valuing their integrity, they have forsaken it in favor of the easy way out. *This* is why they feel bad, and this is also why it is fitting that they feel bad. For this is how they relearn the value of integrity—through being out of integrity and in pain—which is how, with any luck, all of us, at any age, relearn it.

Context Is Everything

In this story, Zoe does not *quite* seem to be cheating, but something is going on with that e-mail that troubles her mom, and perhaps Zoe herself. Academic dishonesty is a pressing problem in many schools and for many families, and it is a very rare child indeed who will not be tempted at some point. In the middle school years, and certainly before, children have a strong and clear grasp of right and wrong. By the time they reach high school, these same kids may well report an increasing pressure to cheat, to gain grades they don't deserve, or to fulfill assignments they believe they cannot fulfill without cheating.

Now, when Zoe is in the sixth grade, Marsha has a chance to anticipate a lot of these problems. Moral crises hardly ever arrive in neat packages, and certainly by the time our children are teenagers, they will be able to see all the gray areas. What we have here is an opportunity for this parent and her child to talk through the issues in advance.

If we take everything that Zoe says at face value (and there seems no compelling reason, based upon the evidence we have, to do otherwise), she is not aiding and abetting, technically, someone who is cheating. At the same time, she is tacitly approving of, it seems, somebody else's less than scrupulous behavior. Whatever may be driving Lizzy, whatever she is up to ultimately, she is in effect doing something that she should not be doing. And that means Zoe is implicated, or will be, by being at the very least a participant in a culture of dishonesty. Can Zoe grasp this point? Yes. In fact, she needs to act upon that understanding, by rejecting that culture of dishonesty, because her integrity is under siege.

From another vantage point, the practice of academic dishonesty begins quietly and insidiously, gaining momentum if left unchecked. For instance, cheating on a homework assignment is usually where a pattern of cheating begins. It's easy to get away with and easier to rationalize: *I put in the time. I just didn't get it, so why should I be penalized? I mean I met the spirit of the assignment.* The danger here is that, undetected, it is a small step from there to composing a cheat sheet for a test. It is an even smaller step from browsing the Internet for information to cutting and pasting whole paragraphs composed by others and claiming them as their own work. (In middle school and high school, this is the current fashion; it will not work as well in college, where professors routinely employ sophisticated software designed to compare submitted papers with on-line resources.)

The interesting thing about cheating in schools is that more often than it seems likely, kids wander into cheating or find themselves in relationships with other kids who themselves justify cheating. Kids can have some very high-minded reasons, believe it or not, to cheat. Some will cheat to help a friend who is struggling in a certain subject to get the good grade to get into the "good" high school, so they can attend together. Will Lizzy one day call upon Zoe to "help" her with homework to reciprocate for all the "help" she is sending her way? There's a chance verging upon a probability that may well happen.

Chances are also excellent, though, that Zoe is going to realize, simply by virtue of her mom's taking this event seriously, that cheating can be found at the bottom of a slippery slope, the one she is sliding down, whether she wants to admit it or not. And that recognition might give her the wherewithal to initiate a conversation with Lizzy that at this point seems much too difficult to broach. Maybe in the effort to explain herself to Lizzy, however, she will make her own values clear to herself.

But Just to the Left of Center . . .

In this story, it is tempting to pay exclusive attention to what at first glance seems like a possible case of cheating. As events progress, whether Zoe cheated or not becomes fuzzy, and shocking as it may seem, less important to her integrity than the way she conducts her relationship with Lizzy.

Zoe is risking her integrity with Lizzy, and this is something that she almost recognizes, but not quite. She needs her mom's help to see it. That is, Zoe seems uncomfortable in her relationship with Lizzy and with the way each of them characterizes it differently. Zoe pities Lizzy, while Lizzy considers Zoe a friend. The integrity issue for Zoe is that she knows that Lizzy's perspective on their relationship is erroneous, and whether Zoe intends to or not, she supports Lizzy's understanding by accepting her "HOMEWORK" e-mails, even intermittently commenting on them. Effectively, Zoe is lying to Lizzy.

Probably the first time Lizzy sent an e-mail with a homework attachment Zoe was flabbergasted, unsure of how to respond. Did Lizzy think that Zoe would cheat? Did Lizzy think that Zoe needed to cheat? Did Lizzy think that she was smarter than Zoe? Was Lizzy desperately seeking a friend? Probably all of this, and more, flashed through Zoe's mind in full color upon receiving that first e-mail. But now, further along in their correspondence, these e-mails elicit nothing but complacency in Zoe, and this is the problem. For complacency, just like expediency, is a marker of being out of integrity—something *both* children and parents need to remember.

Zoe is probably right that the homework attachment is just Lizzy's way of trying to make a friend. Furthermore, because Zoe does not use the information sent her, she thinks she is not being unethical. But that initial discomfort she experienced with that first e-mail is not gone, it's just been pushed to the side by her intellectualization of what Lizzy is doing. Practically speaking, she is out of integrity and no longer uncomfortable being so. She has adapted to being out of integrity with herself in her relationship with Lizzy. This is the "something's wrong here" that Marsha feels at the end of her conversation with Zoe but is at first unable to articulate.

Before proceeding, however, let us be crystal clear on one point: Few if any parents in Marsha's position would be capable of recognizing the integrity issue hiding in the corner. Most of us would jump all over the cheating because we knew something was amiss, and with no other explanation available, that would seem like the best bet. We can all learn from Marsha: Recognize a problem, get away for a while to clear our heads, and then reengage with our new understanding. And as parents, we have more than ample opportunity to practice walking away, scratching our heads a while, and then walking back to the situation at hand. In other than the most straightforward situations—don't put your hand on the hot burner, do chew your food before you swallow, always look both ways before crossing the street—nothing is usually obvious in the art of parenting.

The Next Conversation

When mom and daughter talk again, Marsha will need to take the lead in refocusing the integrity issue. Now the discussion should be about being whole and genuine in relationships, in particular, in Zoe's association with Lizzy. Marsha needs to help Zoe see that when she misrepresents herself, even if she thinks it is for the good of the other, she does both parties a disservice. For Zoe, that means she loses full access to her spontaneity, creativeness, and empathy when she is with Lizzy. On the other side, Lizzy loses the opportunity to develop a real friendship or to look in the mirror and discern how she needs to change in order to have true friendship. Most important, when children consciously or unconsciously fake friendship, they learn to ignore or mistrust their own intuition, which is an internal guide to their integrity.

Zoe learns to ignore her intuition that something is wrong about accepting Lizzy's e-mails and pretending they are appreciated. Lizzy comes to discount her intuitions that her friendship with Zoe is not quite a friendship because on the surface they seem to be acting like friends—they are intimate coconspirators flouting school rules about cheating. But that doesn't lead to friendship, and they are not friends. Somehow, Marsha needs to get all this across to Zoe. Not all at once, but eventually.

So what is Zoe to do, and how can Marsha be of assistance to her daughter in advance of any forthcoming problem? Let's begin by considering what she didn't do, and what she shouldn't do.

Marsha herself did not take the expedient route. She did not decree: No more e-mails from Lizzy, or no more e-mails, period. She also did not decree: No more dealings with Lizzy from here on out. These tactics in the short run would "solve" one aspect of the problem, but they would leave ignored the real problems, which involve Zoe's coming to terms with her relationships and taking responsibility for what she does as well as what she does not do. Ruling out these options, then, what else can Marsha do? Plenty.

Zoe's mother can shape the conversation with her daughter by asking her questions about her relationship with Lizzy, and what she supposes Lizzy thinks she is doing by volunteering her this work. In addition, Marsha needs to press her daughter to investigate what she is gaining by *not* confronting Lizzy, by *not* making clear that she is not interested in seeing this work. She might even ask Zoe if she needs help in sending this message to Lizzy. She will certainly want to know what Zoe means when she says that Lizzy is needy for friendship. What else would Zoe do to further this illusion? With Lizzy or with somebody else? What wouldn't she be willing to do? She might even wonder to what extent it is true that Zoe herself is fearful of losing a connection with somebody by stating and living up to her own moral limits.

Finally, when Zoe says that she is unwilling to hurt her classmate's feelings, is she really indicating that she is avoiding a necessary confrontation? Here is a chance to underscore another crucial dimension of integrity. Being in integrity means sometimes, if not always, standing up and speaking your mind, even if it makes you uncomfortable or unpopular in the short term. That is why we as parents will applaud every single time our kids take the unpopular position, either at home or at school or anywhere else. It means that when push comes to shove, they will be less afraid to resist the pressures of conformity, for the desire to conform always compromises our integrity.

GOODNIGHT, HONEY: PARENTING 202

As he settled into his side of the bed, Bob turned to Marsha. "So, how did we do with our homework tonight, Mom?"

"I give you a B–, maybe C+. I get an Incomplete. We'll see what Zoe comes back with. We've got one kid struggling with being herself in a friendship and another with low expectations of himself."

It was the lowest grade Bob ever received, but he said it was fair, and besides, he had a crush on the teacher. Then he said, "It's hard being a fourth-grader—that's what I found out going over all that homework. I had kind of an epiphany. Pete's working harder than I thought, and that stuff isn't easy. There's still a lot of room for improvement."

Marsha turned over. "For you, too. Maybe for both of us. But let's not forget Pete's in the fourth grade."

"You're right. And then again, we've got one kid whose curiosity and persistence will bring her enormous successes and another whose playfulness and sense of balance will keep him in good stead no matter what comes his way."

"Nice to know you see that side, too. Keep this up, and you'll be getting a B."

"All in all, just another typical Tuesday night."

"Only thing is, typical is more messy and complicated than we ever thought."

"Think our parents worked this hard?" Bob asked.

Marsha didn't reply. She was asleep.

nine

Sportsmanship

What Can My Child Learn About
Integrity from Competition?

If winning isn't everything, why do they keep score?

—Vince Lombardi

Yes, victory is sweet, but it doesn't necessarily make life any easier the next season or even the next day.

—Phil Jackson, *Sacred Hoops*

IT'S NOT HOW YOU PLAY THE GAME?

It was a beautiful spring day, and it wasn't even spring. The sky was clear, the sun shone brightly, and the soccer field and three rows of bleachers were dry. Alicia couldn't think of any place she'd rather be, watching her daughter play a game she loved.

Alicia saw Ella at midfield. Ella smiled and gave her mom a quick wave. Alicia knew that such displays were on their last legs. After all, Ella was ten, and fast approaching thirteen, to tell by the conversation about boys Alicia had overheard when driving the car pool. But there was still a lot of time for mother-daughter bonding, at least that's what she kept telling herself. Besides, she

159

thought, or hoped, she had read somewhere that teenage girls from divorced families tended to stay closer, and nicer, to their mothers than kids from nondivorced families. She was counting on it.

This was the first game Alicia had attended since Ella moved up to the Senior Soccer League. Most of the games were right after school, and usually Alicia could not afford the time away from work, at least in the middle of the day. She missed the old league, where games were scheduled only on weekends. But this was a rare weekend game, and Ella had made her promise to be there. In fact, Ella had said "please" in that four-year-old way of implying that this one was important. Alicia needed no convincing. There was no way she would have missed the game.

Some of her best memories were of watching Ella in the Pee Wee Soccer League, where she had been a real star. It had been a tough call whether or not to allow Ella to move up from Pee Wee to Senior Soccer, but all the coaches, other parents, and Ella herself had assured her that it was a great opportunity. Still, Ella was the only ten-year-old on the squad, and Alicia wasn't 100 percent settled in the decision, if for no other reason than wanting to be able to attend more of the games herself.

Funny how the decision to play Senior Soccer kept replaying in Alicia's mind. Unlike last year, Ella wasn't as eager to go to practice and she wasn't pounding the ball against the back of the garage after school. Speaking of last year, it seemed like the first thing Ella did upon getting home each day was to shed her school clothes and put on her Pee Wee uniform, game day or not. She was proud to wear it around the house and the neighborhood. But this year, Alicia saw the "12" jersey only on game day. This change surprised Alicia, but she chalked it up to shyness around the older kids.

The other moms and dads greeted each other by name; some even saved seats for one another. Times like this made Alicia feel isolated as a single, working mom in suburbia. She thought of screwing up her courage and introducing herself to the others, but after a long week at the office, she decided to cut herself some slack and watch the game in anonymity. Perhaps Ella felt the same disconnection with her new teammates.

The first half of the game was exciting and ended with Ella's team, the Gaels, down 3-1. Even though it's a cliché to say so, the game was closer than that. Ella had played about ten minutes in the first half, enough for Alicia to realize what a difference there was between ten and twelve. Whereas in Pee Wee Ella had been the strongest and fastest player in almost every game, here in Senior Soccer she was consistently a step behind the other girls. Her instincts were right there, but physically she lagged. Alicia sympathized with her daughter as she realized that this lag was a function of age and not talent. And the other girls seemed to make no big deal of it, other than the star of the team, Lillian, who shook her head when Ella messed up, and even yelled at her a couple of times. To be honest, Lillian did this with all the players, not just Ella. But nothing like this ever happened in Pee Wee. The coach, who looked to be in her early twenties, seemed to know the game and seemed to be supportive of the kids, though she never did tell Lillian to back off Ella, or anyone else.

As the second half began, another parent joined the group.

"What did I miss? Are we winning?"

"Hey, Jack, where you been?"

"What's the score?"

They told him but said the team was playing well.

"We need this game." And then, reaching into the cooler he had carried in under his arm, he offered OJ and bagels.

"Wouldn't be a Gael game without some of Jack's Snacks."

"I've seen this team play before," he said. "I know we're better than they are. We've got to pull it together this half."

Alicia groaned over the use of the first person plural. Talk about a lack of boundaries. But then again, her ex had assured her that she had no problems keeping boundaries.

"Who scored for us?"

"Lillian, of course."

Jack couldn't hold back the smile. That's when Alicia saw the same jaw line and same smile as Lillian. This was Lillian's dad.

As he took off his jacket and walked toward the sidelines and the team bench, Alicia saw the big, bold typeface on the back of his T-shirt:

It's Our Time!
July 10, 1999

She had no idea what it meant, but her stomach began to flutter.

Jack made his way to the sidelines where the girls seemed to recognize him, at which point he simultaneously admonished and encouraged them. Alicia had no idea how he was doing both at the same time, but he was. The coach was now relegated to knocking the loose balls into the oversized net bag.

Ten minutes into the second half, the score was tied 3-3. Jack seemed to be having an effect on the players. He was having an effect on Alicia, too. She was disgusted at his behavior, and she knew exactly where Lillian got her attitude.

"C'mon, Gail, you could have had that pass. Way to go, Sheila! Good hustle. If everyone worked that hard, we'd be up by five goals. Hey, ref, you gonna blow that whistle or just hold it between your lips all afternoon? Coach, why the hell do you have *her* taking the free kick? There's only a few minutes left. No, no, no, you can't leave *her* in now!"

That "her" Jack referred to was Ella. Alicia was, she realized, for the first time in her life, speechless. And it only got worse.

The coach shrugged her shoulders. "You know the rules. Everybody plays."

"But not now, the score is tied. We need this one."

But by then the coach had turned her back on Jack and was yelling to one of her players to get into position. Alicia also saw that her daughter had heard Jack's every word. Ella looked on the verge of tears. Alicia found herself pulling harder for her daughter than she could ever remember before.

Then it happened. One of the opposing players stole the ball from Ella and knocked her flat on the grass. Ella struggled to her feet as Jack's voice boomed, "Hey, Number 12, get up and get the ball back. Don't make it worse by quitting."

Right now, with another parent berating her daughter, Alicia couldn't find her voice, let alone put together a coherent sentence.

Then it was Lillian's turn. "Ella, if you touch the ball again, just pass it to me. You can't dribble through these guys."

Strange, but even though there were ten players on the bench, the coach, the opposing team's players, the referees, and plenty of parents rooting for their children, Alicia could only hear what Lillian and her dad were saying to her little girl.

Then, in the bat of an eye, Ella was tackling an opposing player as she attempted to steal the ball. To call it a tackle would be an understatement. Ella was out of control.

The referee was right there. "Foul, Number 12." And then, "Penalty kick."

Jack's roar could be heard throughout the park. "Get your head out of your ass! It was a good tackle. Are they paying you for this home-job or what?"

"That's a bad call, ref. She's just doing what everyone else is doing." Alicia scarcely recognized her own voice. That's when Jack turned toward her and raised his fist in support.

"I did not foul her!" Ella was protesting on her own behalf. Her coach was telling her to calm down, that, indeed, it was a good call.

"It was a terrible call! Whose side are you on?" Jack was in his element.

Then Alicia heard her precious daughter utter something to the referee that she never imagined escaping Ella's lips. The ref heard it, too. Within seconds she was pulling out the red card and pointing Ella to the bench. She had just been ejected. Worse, her team was now down one player for the rest of the game.

Now Jack changed his tune. "C'mon, 12," he yelled. "Hold it together. You can't lose it every time someone makes a bad call. Stop thinking of yourself and think of the team. Grow up."

Jack had told Alicia's daughter to grow up. For the first time this morning, she agreed with him.

NOTES HOME

One day, all of us will witness our children doing something heretofore unimaginable. Throwing a tantrum in the toy store, refusing to get dressed in the morning, knocking another child down on the playground and laughing about it: We will look at our children with frightful wonder and ask ourselves, "Where did I go wrong?" It's a natural enough feeling. It's just not the best question.

Ella's outburst is something Alicia never saw coming. But before we can understand how to respond to such an incident, we need to reflect upon the underpinnings of what Ella has done. After all, occurrences like this are never random, and they can furnish occasions for honest talk, insight, and change. Both mom and daughter have a lot of work to do here, and it's worth all the effort they will expend. Alicia needs to stay focused on Ella's growth, and Ella needs to grasp the increasing complexity of her life.

How Children Communicate

Through the years, we are all impressed with how direct our children are with us in most of their communications. "No, I don't want that toy. I want this toy." Or "Mommy, will you please help me do this?" Or "My tummy hurts. I think I'm going to throw up." These are all clear calls to action—especially that last one.

A child's directness is a tonic. Yet over the years, we have come to realize that while most of the time they are direct, they are, at other times, maddeningly indirect. Your boy's crying over a make-believe "Ow-ie" is his way of saying, "Stop paying so much attention to my little sister. How about me?" Or your daughter's headache at seven in the morning is transparent in its attempt to cover up for failing to complete a homework assignment.

As parents, we learn over the years how to translate our children's indirectness. Using our intuition and relying upon our experience, we become facile at understanding the meaning behind these circuitous communications. That is, we sense that there is more going on than meets the eye. Call it a feeling, a hunch, or a gut instinct, but it's there. Something about their voice, or their movements, or their overall demeanor alerts us to look again. Only more closely this time.

Alicia has noticed changes in Ella since Pee Wee. (She's not wearing her uniform around the house, and she voices a childlike "please" when asking her mom to come to the game.) Alicia paid attention. She did not know what was up, but she did know something was amiss. Once she was at the game and saw what was happening with Ella and her Senior Soccer team, she could begin to piece together Ella's clues. In short, for reasons her daughter was unable to express, Ella was in over her head.

In retrospect, it seems plausible that Ella has been uncomfortable all along as a member of the Gaels. For one thing, she is no longer the star. In fact, she has become someone the star of the team criticizes whenever the opportunity arises, which, given the age differences, is probably often.

Two forces are pushing down on Ella now. One has to do with self-assessment. Kids go through life adjustments all the time, as they appraise their progress in art, in performance, in academics. This is normal, difficult, and good. Few kids will be stars every year of their lives. This is part of growing up, adjusting to changing realities and status. Parents need to walk a fine line here, between encouraging their kids to try harder and encouraging their kids to acknowledge both their strengths and weaknesses. Unless we are careful and clear, we will promote sour grapes and disparagement of others' accomplishments, or we will push our kids beyond their capabilities, which leads to injury or disillusionment, or both.

The second force is Ella's isolation. In a sense, she is alone on this team, without another ten-year-old peer. That disconnection, coupled with the new reality of her diminished role as a player, is a recipe for resentment, which is exactly where she is headed when she is thrown out of the game.

Even worse, she has a coach who abandons her emotionally to the insensitivity of the star's father. This coach's job is to take care of her players, which means adopting a variety of roles, from cheerleader to critic to teacher to protector. She should be exhorting Ella to give more of herself, and she should be praising her for her good efforts. She should also be teaching her new skills to improve her play, and she should be shielding her from destructive criticism—from another player, coach, referee, or parent. Ella's coach has let her down.

At ten years old, what Ella is enduring from Jack—and to a degree from Lillian, too—borders on emotional abuse, something all coaches must protect their players from. As we will discuss, the beauty of athletics is that they can teach participants invaluable life lessons. Participants have the opportunity to learn about compassion, loyalty, perseverance, and teamwork. Once the adults around them, however, try to motivate players through embarrassment or humiliation, they only succeed in shaming the participants and tainting their pure joy in the sport.

How Your Child's Intuition Is a Guide

In this story, the good news for Alicia is that she can immediately focus on Ella's integrity. The consequences Ella experienced during the game—the red card, penalty kick, loss of her teammates' esteem—have occurred naturally and dramatically. Ella requires little else from her mom other than underscoring that aggressively tackling an opponent and mouthing off to a referee is unacceptable, and not because Alicia is personally mortified and embarrassed but because this is not who Ella is or wants to be. So what matters here are not the social consequences but the more private, internal ones.

It is easy to envision another parent, in similar circumstances, getting lost in embarrassment and missing the opportunity to help her child learn to explore and value her integrity. Yelling and hair pulling in this situation would only distract from the real work at hand. This is the difference between a parent acting as a loving and compassionate teacher and one who acts as an enforcer of social convention.

For all of us, children especially, our intuition alerts us to being out of integrity. Our intuition is that nagging feeling that something is wrong; it is that voice that tells us to think again; and it is that unease that does not let us enjoy our victories or learn from our losses. If the Gaels end up winning the game, chances are that Ella's intuition will not let her enjoy the fruits of her labors. In general, Ella is out of integrity as a member of the team. Bad sportsmanship, either in winning or in losing, points to a lack of integrity.

Alicia's objective here must be to help Ella make the connection between her integrity and intuition. That is, Ella's intuition has lots to say about the state of Ella's integrity if she can pay attention. This is critical. This is how Ella learns to trust herself and to be her own best guide in difficult situations. (As the future parent of a future teenager, Alicia can regard this as her best bet for safeguarding her daughter against the tempestuous reality of adolescence. If integrity is important to Ella as a child and if she trusts her intuition to keep close tabs on her integrity throughout childhood, then she will not go far astray during adolescence.)

As is true with most worthwhile learning, Alicia can only point Ella in the direction of this connection. She cannot hand it over to her in any neat packages or high-minded lectures. No, the connection is made through questions, reflection, and hard work. That is, Alicia will ask Ella questions that Ella will be unable to answer. They require her to go think about them for a while. (And they don't necessitate that she check in with her mom once she's reached any conclusions. What her intuition has to say about her integrity may be beyond words for a long time. In the long run, Alicia will understand the conclusions Ella has drawn more by watching her daughter's behavior than by anything she says.)

At the same time, Alicia needs to let Ella know where she stands. She should disapprove of Ella's behavior, but she needs to make sure that she isn't so high on her horse that she is out of Ella's view. Our kids understand our smallest nuances, so chances are that even before Alicia utters a word, Ella knows how her mom feels. Still, Alicia must speak those words. Ella needs to hear them and to remember them, because when she reflects on the questions her mom is going to ask, her mom's thoughts and feelings will provide an essential backdrop for her overall understanding. Here are some of the questions Alicia might consider broaching:

- How do you feel about getting red-carded?
- Is winning the most important thing for you?
- Are you enjoying soccer this year?
- How is soccer different in Senior versus Pee Wee?
- Whom are you really angry at?
- After you tackled that girl, what were you feeling inside?
- You know that voice of intuition I always talk about—what was it saying to you while all of this was going on?
- What do you think about what you said to that referee? Is there anything you wish you could change?
- What does all this say to you about playing for the Gaels?

Most important, and most difficult, is that after Alicia asks each of these questions, she must stay committed to listening to all that Ella has to say. She must allow for silences so that Ella can, in her own way, unpack her conflicting emotions. Pragmatically, this might mean that one question may be enough to unlock the door to Ella's thoughts and feelings.

Athletics and Character

Do athletics build character, as ardent supporters of sports claim? The answer is a great big fat *maybe*. Moral and ethical strength may be an outcome of a successful athletic program, but then again, the opposite may also occur. It is not sports by themselves that develop character, it's the people who play, coach, watch, and organize the sports. And remember, parents are not only their children's first teachers but also their first coaches and referees.

What matters most is the intent of the program, team, and coach, and that speaks to how success is defined. If games won and lost are the only criteria, then character development is an unlikely by-product. If, however, success is defined as perseverance, honesty in dealing with teammates, subordinating personal goals for the betterment of the team, and explicitly developing character, then character can be an outcome. As Jim Thompson, author and founder of the Positive Coaching Alliance, writes, "'Effort goals' are much more motivating than 'outcome goals.' The latter depend on the quality of the opponents. Effort goals are within reach of any athlete who tries hard, regardless of the opposition's talent."[1]

At the heart of the matter, though, is that we cannot forget we are talking about children here. It was Jean Piaget who stressed that the work of childhood is play. If we, as parents, lose sight of this, so will our children. If games, or recitals or performances, for that matter, are grim, competitive, joyless affairs, then our kids lose out. If you hear a coach talking about your ten-year-old getting a college scholarship, run away—and join another team or league!—for that coach has lost perspective, and if you're not careful, so will your child. (This is different from a coach's telling a parent that her daughter is an outstanding athlete and will probably garner much success and satisfaction from athletics as she gets older.) At bottom, a parent's job is to make sure that fun and play remain part of the athletic program. And that is not as easy as it sounds. There are a lot of Jacks in the world.

What's wrong with being Jack? After all, he seems to love his daughter. He seems to support the team. Go to any Little League game and you will see Jacks, and Jacquelines, too. Jack could be thinking that he is motivating his daughter to play harder and that he is encouraging the team to win. But in reality, he's crossed two lines here: He's taken the joy away from play, and he's missed the point that for young children, it should not be all about winning.

Even in some six- and seven-year-old leagues, where nobody keeps official score, the kids know by game's end which team has won. This means, therefore, that we do not have to teach them to value winning over losing; it is natural. We do, however, have to remind them to have a good time, to stand by their teammates when the going gets rough, to savor the well-executed play, and to acknowledge when someone has outplayed you—and learn from that example how to do better next time. The beauty of this is that whatever the result on the scoreboard, there can be a positive experience on both sidelines and on everybody's ride home.

THE RIDE HOME

Alicia and Ella had been in the car a few minutes when Alicia broke the awkward silence that hung between them.

—That was pretty awful out there.

—I can't believe the ref threw me out. It was a clean tackle.

—Honey, I'm no soccer expert, but you clobbered that girl.

—You're right, you're no expert.

—What's wrong with you? I've never seen you like this around soccer before.

—Soccer's no fun anymore. I wish I was still playing Pee Wee.

—You can if you want to.

—I don't know what I want. I just want soccer to be fun again. I hate getting yelled at. I hate not being as good as the other girls.

—Coach seems like a nice person.

—Maybe that's part of the problem. She's too nice.

—Oh, you're talking about Lillian's dad?

—Lillian, too.

—They do seem a little extreme.

—All they do is yell, especially at me. I hate it.

—Have you said anything to them?

—Mom! Are you crazy? She's the best player on the team and everyone loves her dad. He's the one that brings sodas and chips after the game. Besides, he just wants what's best for us.

—Best for you? Yelling at players, swearing at referees, you call that best?

—He wants us to learn to be tough. He says it's tough being a girl these days. He says women can do anything men can do. Which, when you think about it, is actually stupid. We can do way more. No guy ever had a baby.

—Do you want to learn to be tough in the way Lillian's dad says?

—Yeah, sure. I don't want to be a baby.

—There are different kinds of tough, you know. It's not always about winning. Like trying your best and respecting the other players; like valuing your best efforts whether you win or lose; like supporting your teammates rather than yelling at them. Understand?

—Not really.

—Remember that inner guide or voice we always talk about—your intuition? What does that have to say about that tackle and what you said to the referee?

—Kind of stupid. I'm sorry I swore at him, Mom. It's the first time I ever said anything like that.

—It's not OK, but I understand. I think from here on out you need to pay more attention to your intuition around soccer than what everyone is yelling at you.

—Wish it were that easy.

—Want some help?

—I guess.

—Ever hear of Vince Lombardi, the football coach?

—No.

—Anyway, he once said, "In great attempts it is glorious even to fail." I like that better than some of the other things he said.

—I like that, too.

—Thought you would. We can put it on your bulletin board if you like. Oh, by the way, what the heck happened on July 10, 1999?

—Mom. What planet are you from? Women's World Cup? We beat China in free kicks. Remember? We watched it together. That was awesome.

Rethinking an Old Decision

No two kids are the same; we all know that. There are times, however, when we are asked to make decisions based on some of their differences, to declare that our child is unlike others in a specific arena, often one where they have natural talent. We help them decide whether or not to skip a grade, for instance, or to move up with the older kids in the music lessons, or to move up to an older, more competitive team in athletics. During these moments, we ask ourselves a range of questions in which we speculate about the future based on what we know in the present. *Where will she be the happiest? Is this the right challenge for her now? What is the downside? Will she stand out too much? Am I pushing too hard to let her take the challenge? Am I being too protective?* These are important considerations, and, of course, there are no right answers or guaranteed results.

Few decisions are ever final. We and our children make decisions, live with the results, and then decide whether to continue along one path or another. In this regard, most of our decisions are experiments in action. This is how our kids learn to make better and better decisions. And we serve them by moving slightly to the side and by keeping our attention focused on their integrity. Think of it this way: We will not always be present and available when our children need help making a decision, especially when they get older. The time to teach them how to make decisions based on their integrity is when they are children. Therefore, when we speak of decisionmaking in children, we are really talking about collaboration, experimentation, and parental influence.

Many parents in Alicia's shoes would reconsider their initial decision to let their daughter play in the Senior Soccer League in the first place instead of staying another year in the Pee Wee Soccer League. This is not a bad idea, as long as the daughter is involved in the decision making. And her participation is the key to making and remaking these decisions. That way, there is no such thing as a bad decision—only decisions that work out and others that help you to assert your integrity and incorporate previous experiences into a deeper part of yourself.

A Parent's Intuition

Parents do well to trust their own intuition around their children. When it comes to health, safety, behavior around the house, or attitudes with friends, parents are seldom far off the mark when they trust their intuitive hunches. But too many of us ignore these glimmers of insight in the name of proof. We are to a large extent a litigious society, which means that we look for blame and find fault instead of analyzing what is happening right before our eyes. We tend to wait until we have evidence of a wrongdoing, a letdown, a failure, a disappointment before we act on our suspicions. With our children, this time lag almost always amounts to a mistake.

Our children are best served when we don't wait and we trust what we are feeling. Our intuition is usually enough: "I can't put my finger on it, but it just doesn't seem like you are enjoying soccer like you used to. Is there anything I should know?" This kind of approach works across the board. "You don't seem real happy about getting the A on that project you did with Eric. Is there something bothering you?" Or: "It didn't seem like you and Timmy played together much at the park today. Is there something wrong between the two of you?" These are inquiries based on our observations and clear-eyed knowledge of our children. Asking these kinds of questions is what makes the world safe for our children. They know they are being seen for who and what they are, good and bad, which leads to their doing better and valuing their integrity even more.

Alicia knew something was wrong with Ella, but she failed to recognize that she was aware of this until she attended the game. She could have missed this for many reasons, ranging from the stress in her own life to a general reluctance to see a problem with her daughter that she would need to confront. Whatever the reason, once the issue of Alicia and soccer is taken care of, Alicia needs to ask herself how she missed the distress in her daughter for so long. This is not an exercise in guilt. Instead, this is how she forges her own integrity as a parent and how she comes to relearn who her daughter is, over and over again. Parents are never omniscient. We all have our limits. There is only one consolation, and that is whatever our limits, we always have our own integrity and intuition to guide us—and our children.

ten

The Shock of Emerging Sexuality

How Can I Underscore Integrity Even While My Child Is Growing Up So Fast?

On an afternoon two years ago my life veered from its day-in day-out course and became for a short while the kind of life that can be told as a story—that is, one in which events appear to have meaning. . . . Supposedly, your hair stands on end in the instant before you get struck by lightning. I had a similar sensation that afternoon. . . .

—**Josephine Humphreys,** *Rich in Love*

FEATURE ATTRACTION AT THE MULTIPLEX

–One–

Emily's dad had a question. "Now, what time does the movie end again?"

"Four-thirty. Same as the first two times you asked. We'll meet you at the side exit, on Chestnut right after. You sure you don't mind driving Ninaryl home after?"

He was momentarily confused, until he figured out that Emily was referring to the dynamic duo of Nina and Cheryl—Ninaryl—her best friends. "Very cute. You have money?"

She said, for the third time as well, that she did.

"Mom and I will be home if you need anything. You have the cell phone?"

"Yes, Dad, yes, a thousand times yes. Don't worry, OK? See you after the movie. Love ya!" It was pouring, and Emily leaped out of the car to run toward Cheryl and Nina, waiting in their identical green ponchos under the theater marquee. It was the third straight day of heavy rain, and everybody was getting a case of cabin fever. Emily assumed that was why her father volunteered to drive her to meet her friends at the Saturday matinee.

But almost immediately, she felt sorry she hadn't given him a peck before taking off. She hoped his feelings weren't going to be hurt. He was a little touchy these days, and things like that were happening more and more often to her.

"Have fun, Emily," her dad said to himself after she slammed the car door shut. Sitting there, hands on the steering wheel, watching the wipers as they whooshed across the windshield, he had a sinking realization. He had better grow accustomed to the changes that awaited him. There he was, having said good-bye to his daughter as she rushed off with friends to explore a much bigger world. But was that the way to think about it? She was acting sometimes like a teenager, even though she was only eleven years old. Was she somehow a teenager already? The other day, somebody on the radio had been talking about "tweens"—eight- to twelve-year-olds. That had to be the dumbest made-up word he'd ever heard. And yet something was going on with girls these days. They seemed to be growing up too fast. The things they said, the music they listened to, the clothes they wore, the clothes they didn't wear. Of course, that wasn't true of Emily.

What made it even more complicated was that to look at Emily, you could never tell she was eleven. As she stood next to Ninaryl,

she looked like their older sister rather than one of the Three Mus-
keteers of the Sixth Grade that she was proud to be. Most people
would probably think she was closer to fifteen.

Emily's parents had dealt with this unsettling issue a few months
ago when they had a very good, very clear talk about—well, it was
hard to label what they had talked about. Her precocity? Her sexuality? Her maturity? The problem was, Emily looked so grown up
that they were worried that older kids—especially the older boys—
might treat her in ways that would make her uncomfortable. Still,
they managed to get through that conversation, and they reasoned
they now had a head start on helping her handle any complicated
situations that might conceivably arise.

OK, he thought to himself, *we did the right thing and Emily's a
good kid, a terrific kid, a sweet kid, a smart kid, a strong kid, and she
knows she has support at home to help her as she grows up. So how come
I still feel anxious and worried?*

Emily's dad slowly drove off, carrying inside the unmistakable
feeling that while Emily was still his little girl, nobody would think
of her as a little girl much longer.

—Two—

The girls waited in what seemed like the longest line in the world.
Had the rain pushed everybody out of their houses today? As they
waited, not very patiently, to hand over their tickets and get their
hands stamped, they couldn't help but notice how cute the ticket
taker was—longish hair, athletic looking, handsome face—and like
most eleven-year-old girls, they joked and giggled about his good
looks. Eventually, they reached the head of the line, at which point
they all slipped into glazed, rapt silence.

"Ticket, please." He received no response. That cute ticket taker
was looking directly at Emily and she was staring back into his
deep brown eyes. "If you want to go to the movie, the way this
works is, I have to get your ticket."

"Oh! Sure." As Emily handed him the ticket, she felt his finger-tips graze her hand. His name tag said he was Phil.

"Ah, Theater Seven. That's a great movie. I've seen it three times myself. You sure you can handle it, though? It's pretty scary." The girls couldn't believe he was chatting with them—it was just amazing—making the people behind them in line wait a little longer.

"We'll be fine." Emily thought it was her responsibility to answer him. He was looking at her, after all.

"If it gets to be too much, let me know and I'll come and rescue you."

The three girls walked into the lobby, took about a dozen measured stately steps, looked back in the direction of the ticket taker, realized he wasn't looking at them, and ran around the corner to Theater Seven. Outside the entrance, they caught their breath and started talking all over each other.

"Emily!" It was Cheryl and Nina squealing at the same time. "He was flirting with you. That was so cool."

"What? No way. He was just teasing me. I mean us."

"He didn't even notice Nina and me. He was flirting with you."

"You think?"

"Definitely."

"You guys are both crazy." And then she laughed and laughed. "I want to see this movie. Come on."

And with that, the girls entered the crowded Theater Seven and found three seats together toward the back. But they could barely sit there, and besides, the coming attractions hadn't even begun yet, so after a few jittery minutes, Nina and Emily decided to get some snacks for all three of them while Cheryl saved their seats. They probably were hungry.

Although actually, Emily was hoping to make some eye contact with Phil, to find out if crazy Ninaryl was right and if maybe he really was flirting with her. He was cute. No boys in her class, heck, no boys in her whole school, were half as cute as Phil.

As they headed toward the snack bar, Emily took a sideways glance to the theater's entrance. She was crestfallen: no Phil. Instead, there was some old guy collecting tickets. He must be at least as old as her dad. She kept studying her shoes, but as she approached the counter, her heart leaped into her throat.

There was Phil, serving up popcorn and making change at the concession stand.

"Oh, it's you again. Movie too scary?"

"Very funny," said Emily. Though how she managed to say anything she had no idea. She heard people refer to having cotton in their mouth. Now she understood what they meant. "It hasn't even started yet."

"Yeah," added Nina, coming to the rescue, filling in the one second of excruciating silence. "Can we get some popcorn and three diet sodas?"

"What would you like?" Phil was staring at Emily.

"I guess some popcorn and a cola."

And turning to Nina. "And how about you?"

"Like I just said a second ago, we'll have one popcorn and three colas."

"Small, medium, or large popcorn? With or without?"

"Large popcorn with butter."

"Tell you a secret," he said, leaning over the glass countertop. "You can have some stale popcorn now, or if you wait a minute, you can have some of the fresh stuff. I recommend waiting."

The girls nodded and Phil, his back to them, filled the three soda cups.

Emily had an idea and addressed Nina. "Why don't you just bring the drinks to Cheryl and I'll wait for the popcorn."

Nina smiled slightly wickedly, nodded, and headed back into the theater.

"So do you go to school around here?" Phil was talking over his shoulder, pretending to attend to the popcorn machine as he spoke with Emily.

"Sure. I go to—sure, I go to school around here."

"You must go to Cathedral because I go to Central and I've never seen you before." Cathedral and Central were the only two high schools in town. "I'd have noticed you."

"Right, I mean no, I don't go to Central."

The three minutes it took for the popcorn to pop felt like a wonderful—a delicious—stretch of eternity. Then, as Phil rang up the order, Emily noticed how he only charged her for a small popcorn, and he definitely winked at her when he did this. It made her feel strange, the winking, sure, but also the ringing up the wrong amount. Her mom would have corrected him on the amount if she were there, though thank God she wasn't. Still, was it her responsibility? Maybe Phil got a discount, or could give discounts to friends, which raised another question. Which was this? Maybe Cheryl and Nina were right. Maybe Phil was flirting. Yet she couldn't completely believe it. Even more surprising, she had to ask herself, was she flirting back at him?

—Three—

"That movie was awesome!"

"No kidding, way better than I thought it would be."

The girls were debriefing one another on the film while making their way out. Nothing new about that. They touched base on everything that ever happened to any one of them. This time there was a difference, though. All Emily could think about was this: Was Phil still working?

As Ninaryl headed for the Chestnut Street exit, Emily floated back into the lobby.

"Hey, Emily. Your dad is going to meet us out here, not out front."

"Oh, yeah, I was just looking around."

"Yeah, right. You're looking for that guy again."

"No, I'm not."

"No, you're not what?" The voice came from behind her, but she recognized it immediately.

"No, I'm not lost. You still working?"

"Yeah, I work until closing tonight."

"Wow. That's a long time." Instantly, she was embarrassed. Had anybody ever said anything half so stupid to a boy half as cute as Phil?

"Yeah, but the boss is all over me so I gotta run. Would it be OK if I called you sometime?"

"Called me?" That was even dumber than her last remark. How do boys and girls actually manage to talk with each other?

"Yeah, you know, on the phone?"

"Uh, sure. I mean, whatever."

"Cool. What's your number?"

"My number?" Part of her wanted to run away right now. Part of her wanted to see how this was going to turn out.

"You know? Your *phone number*? You do have a phone in your house, don't you?"

Just at that moment Emily had a vague recollection of that conversation she had had with her mom and dad a few months ago. She just couldn't remember exactly what it was about, something about how she was growing up.

As she gave him the number, he wrote it on his hand with a ballpoint pen, smiled, and hurried off. He turned back then and put his fist up to his ear as if it were a telephone and winked at her. Emily took this as her cue to get out of there right now.

Outside, in the rain, everybody jumped into the car and Emily just wanted the trip to be over soon so she could sit in her room by herself for a long, long time.

"About time," said Cheryl.

"Where were you?" asked Nina.

Emily smiled at her dad, who smiled in reply and then checked over his shoulder for traffic. She turned to her friends and put her index finger up to her lips.

–Four–

"Emily. Some boy on the phone." Her dad was calling her down the hallway. "He says his name is Phil. You want to talk to him?"

She opened her door and stuck her head around the corner. "Phil? Oh, *Phil*. Oh, yeah, sure. Be there in a sec."

As Emily exited her room, she had a blank look on her face that her dad couldn't miss and she walked breathless along the carpeting as if it were insubstantial as a cloud. Once in the kitchen, though, she scooped up the cordless phone and scampered back to the sanctuary of her room.

This was a first in their home: Emily talking to a boy on the phone, a boy neither her mom nor her dad had ever heard of before.

"Who the heck's Phil?" asked Connie.

"I thought you knew," said Jim.

They were waiting for her twenty minutes later when the "in use" light on the phone finally went dark. It was a very long twenty minutes.

As Emily came into the kitchen to return the telephone, she felt there was an anchor dragging behind her. The weight in the air had to do with the sense that her parents were both fixing their eyes on her from their vantage point on the living-room couch.

"Hey, Emily." Her mom's voice cracked. "Honey, who is Phil? I don't remember ever hearing you mention a Phil before."

"He's a boy I met," she said, moving back to her room.

Dad couldn't help himself. "Wait, wait, wait." He stood up. "Met where?"

"At the movies yesterday."

"How did you meet him?"

"We just started talking. No big deal."

"You meet a boy at the movies, give him our phone number, and talk to him hidden away in your room and you call that no big deal?"

"I thought it was my phone number, too."

"Jim, hold on," said Connie. "What your dad is trying to say is that we're both surprised and maybe a little concerned. Should we be concerned?"

"Really, it's nothing to worry about."

"Good. Then maybe you can tell us a little about Phil."

"Like what?"

"Like, is he in your class?"

"Not really."

"Is he in another grade in your school?"

"Not exactly."

Emily's dad became agitated. "This is the end of Twenty Questions, Emily. Where does this boy go to school and how old is he?"

"I don't know how old he is and I don't exactly remember where he goes to school."

"When did you meet him?"

"Standing in line."

"Did you sit next to him during the movie?"

"No. He had to work." It was too late to take that back and Emily knew it. It was funny, though, how she was both nervous and relieved at the same time.

"Had to work?" He did the math. That boy had to be at least sixteen years old. "So how old is he?"

She could tell that her dad was starting to do his counting to ten, his self-help exercise. "How would I know?"

Her mom jumped back in before things got out of control. "Emily, does Phil know how old you are?"

"I have no idea."

Her dad shouted, "Emily!"

"All right, all right, all right. I didn't tell him, if that's what you're asking."

"Let's be honest. What's your best guess as to how old he thinks you are?"

"He thinks I'm in high school." As Emily said this, she cringed in expectation of her dad's famous temper. But it was weird. This time, no fireworks. She looked up into his face and saw fear instead of anger. Now it was her turn to be surprised.

"What's wrong, Dad?"

He was silent as he kept his eyes focused on the floor.

Her mom spoke instead. "Emily, both your dad and I are surprised, disappointed, and scared by what you are telling us. But I think he and I need some time, alone, to figure out where we go from here. So why don't you hang out in your room for a while, and we'll come get you when we know how to best proceed with this conversation."

"I didn't do anything wrong. I'm sorry."

"We know you are, honey," said her mom, "but that's not what worries us right now. We'll talk in a bit."

NOTES HOME

The Limits of Honesty

Although this occasion feels supercharged (sex will do that in a flash to all of us), it has a great deal in common with most instances when parents and their older, preadolescent children will find themselves drawn into conflict around honesty and integrity.

Certainly, Emily's parents have some urgent points on which to engage their daughter, and because they may well feel an understandable pressure to stress the significance of the moment, they need to slow down and not get swept away by their surging panic. Most important, everyone has to remain involved, and everybody has to keep the talk personal and real. If they don't at least intend to do so, their conversation may conceivably lapse into one extended parental lecture interrupted by Emily's silence and defensiveness, which serves nobody's needs. (After all, she's eleven; that is, she is feisty, self-protective, self-critical, and hypersensitive to everybody else's glaring inadequacies, as well as, sometimes though rarely, her own. We will talk more about being eleven later in this chapter.) The predominant concern has to be for Emily's safety, and her safety is ultimately coupled with a healthy respect for her natural growth. And again, that's *respect* for, not fear over, her emotional, psychological, and social development.

Sexual awakenings are hardly tidy matters. Considering the changes Emily is going through, it would be difficult to imagine that she has much if any conscious control over her inner turbulence and her shifting social identity. That is, she is a sexually precocious (relatively speaking) eleven-year-old girl who is anxious both to explore her feelings and curiosities as well as to maintain connection with her parents. She is a little girl and a budding teenager at the same time, and she wants to keep a firm hold on both worlds. She wants to count on the unconditional love and absolute support of her parents even as she reaches out to a tantalizing world of teenage possibility. Difficult as this is for some parents to appreciate at first, we would not want it any other way. We want her—just as her dad does when he sees her scamper to her friends under the theater awning—to embrace her future and her expanding world of experience.

At the same time, if her parents are wise enough not to employ the notion of integrity as if it were a hammer, they will have a chance to help Emily see the benefits of acting authentically. But the crux of the conversation they are all about to have is that at age eleven with the right guidance from her parents, Emily is capable of appreciating the distinction between honesty and integrity.

Strictly speaking, it should be noted from the outset, Emily never quite lied about her age to Phil, nor did she lie to her parents about what happened at the multiplex. And this is one crucial message for Emily's parents to get across: Not lying is not the same as acting with integrity. To be sure, this is a distinction that is often lost on many adults, never mind their children. Emily is being evasive but not hostile, and certainly not passive—although she is apt to sound simultaneously hostile and passive to somebody not appreciating what she is going through, which is nothing less than a sexual awakening.

Honesty means on one level speaking the truth, which is exactly what Emily did, even though she left lots of ambiguities along the way, together with some implicit nontruths that she hoped would get her through the ordeal. But in developmental terms, most eleven-year-olds become quite literal in how they hear and respond to questions, especially those incisive queries that may leave them feeling vulnerable, if not attacked. This means that Emily answers the exact question asked, no more and no less. The trick here is for her parents to appreciate that she is not being dishonest—for an eleven-year-old.

In Emily's view, she is not dishonest because she has not lied. Her parents sense her evasiveness, though, and they leap to doubt her truthfulness. If Emily and her parents stake these claims, however, they cannot have a productive conversation. Both sides have merit. Emily did not lie, but her parents did not receive full disclosure. What Emily and her parents have in common, though, is Emily's integrity. Emily is uncomfortable, which is a result of her being out of integrity. Her parents sense her discomfort, which they attribute to her move away from integrity. In other words, they now have a starting place for genuine conversation: They can both agree on the state of Emily's integrity.

What's more, if challenged on her honesty, Emily will feel relieved to have a battle to fight that she can win. That's why it's best to sidestep this honesty issue and focus on the deeper meaning of integrity. And because the lens should now be trained on the issue of her being true to herself, and less on the accurate recitation of facts, this means they will be asking a very different set of questions. The questions will be different because they center more on Emily's experience, her authenticity, and her coming to terms with a complicated, indeed earth-shaking, moment.

The Integrity Conversation

All this shows why, once the "facts" are established, and they are confirmed during their short conversation in the kitchen, Emily's parents need to move to the bigger picture, which means deeper and more probing questions. Questions now need to be less about who said what and when and more along these lines:

- How did you feel when you realized he thought you were older than you are?
- How did it feel trying to cover up who Phil was when he called on the phone?
- Do you feel like you represented yourself accurately to Phil?
- If not, how come you didn't try to correct the impression he had?
- Looking back on what happened at the theater, would you do anything different next time?

To put it simply, the idea is to ask questions that cannot be readily answered. No questions that admit, therefore, of a yes or a no answer. Emily's parents need to concentrate on nudging Emily to explore her areas of discomfort during this incident. Then her parents must connect these feelings, doubts, and misgivings to Emily's integrity, which, whether she is conscious of this or not, is her most precious possession. That is, her own incipient sense of integrity is what's behind all the discomfort and it needs to be paid attention to, and if she can bring her own integrity into the light, she will not only be surer as to what she should not or cannot do but sure about what is right and good for her to do.

This parental tact is not designed to instill guilt in her (though insofar as she is still eleven, this may well happen) but instead to help her understand and appreciate the practical underpinnings of integrity in her life. And again, the most direct way for us to take the lessons of integrity to heart is through our being *out of integrity*, which Emily is. Her parents must recognize this and in their own way let these uncomfortable feelings speak for themselves. If they rush to make things right, or even, for that matter, to inflict punishment upon Emily for "lying," they may rob her of the lesson that should be her greatest benefit—the forging of connections, for herself, between her discomfort and her being out of integrity. When Emily's parents gain the sense that Emily is going to be obedient and at the same time true to herself, they can sleep a little easier at night now and in the very immediate future, when in almost no time at all she will be in high school.

For all this to happen, Emily's parents must plant the seeds of exploration, which is why these discussions have to happen over time and not in one sitting. (And by the way, try to make sure everybody is sitting, especially when you feel like launching into a speech when you're standing across the kitchen.) They also have to remain patient, and let the silence accumulate, giving Emily the space and encouragement to explore these bigger issues on her own as well as with them. Practically, this means letting her spend a few hours in her room considering the points her parents brought up or continuing the conversation the next day, after everyone has had a night to sleep on it. For some kids, writing about their experience may even turn out to be a way to make the connection to their integrity.

Once Emily can demonstrate to her parents that she understands how she was out of integrity in her dealings with Phil, and how integrity is indeed crucial to her, she and her parents are free to move on together in examining some of the other issues that arose as a result of this incident. But until the connection to her integrity is cinched, all other discussion is simply moot.

With her parents' helping her draw the line, Emily can affirm limits that she can, at eleven, live with. There may well be resistance to the imposition of parental controls; after all, few kids older than nine have trouble articulating their disappointment over the enforcement of adults' power in their lives. And that's exactly where the emphasis upon integrity comes into play: It is not about externally imposed authority. Emily's parents can insist upon no dating until she is emotionally and psychologically prepared; they can determine that she is not quite ready for a phone relationship (or an on-line dialogue or e-mail relationship) with a sixteen-year-old; they can, at the same time, point to a time not so far down the road when she can date (though for some eleven-year-olds, it will feel like that day will never come).

We believe that kids require appropriate limits. Eleven-year-olds should never go out with sixteen-year-olds. So do not construe our emphasis upon integrity to be tantamount to urging you to cave in. Quite the opposite. If you focus exclusively upon limits, however, you are effectively caving in—to your own fear. Instead, we are suggesting that you explore integrity before, and during, your imposition of realistic, reasonable, respectful limits.

In Emily's case, this is the occasion for her parents to enunciate clearly their position, which probably amounts approximately to this: *No, you can't go out with Phil because you're too young to date and he's simply too old. We do understand why you want to date, though, so now let's begin to look at some of the issues that are going to come into play when you do finally date.* In these kinds of ways, her parents connect her emergent sexuality to her integrity.

Early Puberty in Girls

In 1997, Dr. Marcia Herman-Giddens studied the onset of puberty in 17,000 girls, and her conclusions confirmed what pediatricians were seeing in their offices and parents in their homes: Girls are reaching puberty earlier than previous generations.[1] Herman-Giddens identified two stages of puberty; the second, menarche (menstruation, which marks the formal beginning of puberty in girls), has remained stable since the 1960s at 12.8 years old (and six months earlier in African-American girls). The first stage, the development of secondary sexual characteristics of breast buds and pubic hair, is happening, however, earlier and earlier in girls. Her research estimates that by age eight, 15 percent of Caucasian girls and nearly 50 percent of African-American girls are showing signs of secondary sexual development. At this point, researchers remain unsure as to the causes.

One theory advanced so far relates to obesity. That is, obese girls have been known to develop more quickly than normal-weight children, and since obesity in children between the ages of six and eleven has doubled since the late 1970s, it makes sense that the first stage of puberty would also begin earlier. Another theory relates to chemical pollution in the food chain and air from the use of pesticides, which researchers believe may have increased estrogen activity in young girls. A third theory is that the increased number of sexualized messages that children are subjected to in their daily lives is triggering earlier brain and physical development.

Whatever medical and social explanations are invoked, however, parents are left with little girls who look like teenagers and in many instances are treated like teenagers by older kids and by adults, for that matter. On one level, sexuality is sexuality, and puberty, whenever it explodes, is puberty. But that's not the whole story. Girls are, in effect and on average, sexually more mature than their male peers. This makes for complications that kids in earlier generations never had to cope with. For instance, older boys, teenagers, can find themselves being attracted to younger girls not knowing that they are younger, and these younger girls can find themselves the object of a kind of attention that, as children, they are not quite prepared for. We are not talking about sexual predators, either, though nobody should be naive on this subject when younger and younger children are featured in movies and advertising as sexualized creatures served up for the eroticized attention of the commercial public.

Emily's experience is one example of the complications of early puberty. But remember, for all that, in our story, Phil seems hardly to be a predator of Emily. He is responding, quite naturally, and to him appropriately, to this attractive girl, who seems to him to be much older than eleven. It is easy to believe that once Phil finds out Emily is eleven, he will never call her again. Certainly, if he did keep calling her after learning her age, that would pose a problem of another, graver magnitude, and that is precisely the nightmare Emily's parents are imagining could take place.

One recent area of concern stemming from this uneven development between the sexes is the growing experimentation among children with oral sex. As one educator said, "A lot of eighth-grade girls engage in this activity with high school boys. They see it as a way to please a guy without losing their virginity."[2] This means girls need more information at a younger age about sex and sexuality. Even more important, they need us to make the connection between this type of sexual experimentation and their own integrity. Oral sex to please an older boy is a sign of being out of integrity because it is about a lack of self-worth and authenticity. This behavior, which seems like a shortcut to the acceptance they are naturally searching for, is instead a detour away from the acceptance and power that only they can give themselves or that can only be achieved in a mutual, mature relationship.

The Meaning and Power of Emergent Sexuality — and the Parents' Response

There are some families and some schools that shy away from frank discussion of sex and sexuality on the presumption that such information may well stimulate, if not encourage, sexual activity. We disagree with this position. The research is in, and it is, in fact, unambiguous on these matters. In study after study, we discover that kids who know more about sex—sexuality, disease, condoms, celibacy, and so on—are *less* likely to have sex than those shielded from such information. In addition, those who have that information are more likely to be more responsible in their sexual activity. And of course, that's vital: We do not wish to endanger further our children who are exploring risks. And that is where information can be a lifesaver. In general, it helps to know that our kids are much more savvy and fluent in the vocabulary of the sexual world than we imagine. Therefore, we have an obligation—a moral obligation, we would say—to equip them with the tools (that is, the knowledge) that could well save their lives.

Certainly, however, sex talk is never value-free. How could it be? Parents are the primary educators. So when we tune in to our children's secondary educators (at school, church, doctors' offices), we should listen hard for an emphasis not solely upon disease, danger, and biology but also upon relationships, love, and humanity. And this is another reason that whatever may be going on in our schools and our churches and community centers, nothing replaces our involvement in shaping our children's understanding of one of the fundamentals of their lives: sex and sexuality. And that is also why we need to begin our conversations early on, shaping our dialogue in appropriate ways, building upon our children's own knowledge, questions, and curiosities. Health educators agree that parents can have the greatest influence upon their children in the areas of sex, drugs, and alcohol when they are between the ages of ten and twelve.

Some families may well regard morality as *the* central component of sexuality, while others tend to be relatively agnostic, preferring to see sexual exploration as, if not exactly value-neutral, to some degree value-contingent, and perhaps even inevitable. In extremes, some parents can never see the day coming when their children go out on a date, while others imagine a time when their eventual teenagers, involved in a committed, serious relationship, may well spend the night together in the same room. Still, morality is a major component in the sexuality discussion for most, if not all, families.

In this regard, we would simply urge all parents, of whatever inclination, to acknowledge to themselves the depths of passion in their children and to concede to themselves that perfection and absolute consistency is unattainable by anybody. But whatever parents do—whether they give a green light to sexual exploration or

construct barriers to all choices other than total chastity and absti-
nence—they should be compassionate and pragmatic at the same
time. The way to do this is to ground your relationship, and your
conversation with your kids, in integrity. Despite Hollywood por-
trayals of kids as hedonistic proponents of an R-rated lifestyle,
nothing is further from the truth.

When our children strive to achieve authenticity, they will inevitably struggle with their sexuality and their desires. How could
they not? Sexuality is one of the keys to our humanity. This does
not mean that right and wrong are irrelevant to children and
teenagers. Just the opposite, in fact. Because when they see that
sexuality is a natural and indispensable and treasured part of themselves, they will incorporate it into a larger, more comprehensive
vision of a self. You can just say no to sex, perhaps, but wouldn't it
be better, saner, wiser that at the same time you say yes to who you
are and who you are becoming?

Let us return to Emily. After her first ride around the sexual at-
traction carousel, she is going to feel wobbly not only in her knees
but in her heart. She is going to rethink who she is and begin to
come to terms with who she is becoming, that is, a young woman.
She is going to stare at the objects in her room and wonder if they
still have a place in her life. She is gradually going to connect the
face she sees staring back at her in the mirror with the image she
has of herself, and it's going to take quite a long time before she can
imagine what she looks like to other people, including but not exclusively those cute ones who are staring back at her.

Think back, if you can, to your first brushes with your sexuality.
In particular, what was it like to hold hands for the first time? To
feel flesh against flesh? Or remember the first kisses. The euphoric
feelings that left you floating a few inches above the ground. Once
you tasted those feelings, could you ever have turned back? Emily is
not far from these first experiences, and while her parents may not
be ready for this, they must never lose sight of it either. They have
a lot to do to prepare Emily, and in a small window of time.

Remember that conversation her parents referenced from six months ago, the one about Emily's looking older than her age. That was probably a good talk, but it only set the groundwork for what needs to happen now. They talked to Emily about puberty because she needed to hear about it, but from her point of view, it was an abstract discussion. In all likelihood, she could not connect what her parents were saying to her day-to-day life. Even those weird-sounding discussions of hygiene, even those meetings with her pediatrician, probably felt sort of academic, and remote. But now—after meeting dreamy Phil at the multiplex, after waiting for the magical fresh popcorn, after being asked for her phone number, after getting a call from a high school boy—she certainly can. So her parents need to have that conversation with her again, because she is now capable of understanding how puberty may affect her and those around her. In many ways, her parents need to act as if they never had that earlier conversation because Emily is not the child she was a scant six months ago, and six months ago for an eleven-year-old on the brink of puberty is ancient history.

On Being Eleven

Eleven is a period of attenuation, of feeling stretched out and pulled back and forth. When eleven-year-olds remember how coherent life seemed when they were ten, they feel nostalgic for lost connection and security; and when they contemplate the prospects of twelve and beyond, they feel wistful about a time that seems utterly remote and unattainable. Eleven is a time of *between*: between the past and the future, between heights and depths, between family and friends, between laughter and tears. Speaking of tears, most of your memories of your eleven-year-old may well involve crying—yours and theirs.

Emotionally, one mood seems as right to an eleven-year-old as another. Sometimes they pick and choose and combine them, one from column A, one from column B. Their emotional turbulence relates to the physiological changes of puberty, which is busy re-arranging their internal furniture. Their voices change, for in-stance, which feels quite profound to them, signaling how little control they enjoy over how they express who they are and how they come across to others. Eleven-year-olds can feel betrayed by their growth spurts, especially when they stumble walking across the unimpeded floor.

Intellectually, eleven-year-olds remain fairly concrete in their thinking, but already they are lurching forward, just as likely to track down a book in the library and curl up reading it for hours and hours as they are to complain about the burden of excessive and punitive-seeming homework.

Socially, eleven-year-olds take stock every day, every hour, of their standing in everyone's eyes, feeling under the microscope and vulnerable, or feeling themselves to be observed and ready to per-form for the occasion. "Why are you paying so much attention to everything I do?" is a sentiment that competes with an often un-stated "Watch me and what I'm doing, please." One minute the-atrical, the next secretive, eleven-year-olds keep their parents on their toes for the right cues. Sarcasm comes naturally, as does mum-bling and muttering under the breath in response to an expression of interest. Now and again, you just think you hear some very col-orful language creeping into that wonderfully expanding vocabu-lary. (You thought they never heard you when the hammer came down on your thumb? Or when somebody cut you off on the free-way? Must have been your brother-in-law.)

As important as anything else, however, is the way an eleven-year-old now revalues friends and friendship. Their relationships—almost universally with those of the same sex—suddenly deepen. "Best friend" is a profound designation, and it can apply to one per-son or to a small, exclusive coterie.

For many boys and girls, the onset of puberty, however, causes abrupt shifts in their relationships. Seldom do best friends, or best-friendship groups, arrive simultaneously at puberty. This means that somebody is inevitably left behind. For instance, in Emily's case, we would expect her friendships with "Ninaryl" to become more complicated as she regards them as somehow "younger" than she is. Cheryl and Nina remain, for now, little girls, while Emily becomes attracted to the idea of forming new kinds of relationships. That is, Cheryl and Nina may well be indulging themselves in fantasies of romance with boys whose pictures adorn their walls, but Emily has just had a glimpse of the possibility of a relationship with a real boy. Similar disjunctions take place among boys; some eleven-year-old boys want to talk with their friends about the cute girls in school, while others can't believe there's anything more compelling than throwing the football around or riding their bikes. For instance, one tells a dirty joke and laughs at the punchline, while the other laughs for fear of not laughing—because he doesn't get what's so funny.

For some children, puberty is even more complicated. A significant minority of them realize that, unlike most of their peers, they are attracted to members of the same sex. Gay men and women often comment that it was around this time that they recognized their difference and began their struggle with their own wholeness. It's understandable, in the predominantly heterosexual world, therefore, that they unconsciously sense that their difference precludes not only relationships with many others but a connection with themselves and their own sexuality.

In other words, for all these reasons, eleven can be a time of loneliness and misunderstanding between former best friends as they piece together their new worlds and come to terms with their new bodies and minds. Many of these relationships never recover, sad to say, and this disappointment relates to changes that will take place at home, too. Count on a little bit of regression: They might pull out some toys, they might be underfoot a lot more than before, they might look a little sorrowful. Also count on a little bit of displaced anger, especially in the case of the child left in the dust.

The Storm Before the Quiet Before the Storm

Mothers and fathers also feel the ground shift when their children reach puberty. When the ground stops shaking, in a few years, they look around and see a reconfigured landscape in their homes. In the meantime, moms and sons, moms and daughters, dads and sons, dads and daughters—all are redefining their relationships and interrelationships.

The familiar stereotypes suggest that moms track down their kids and that dads vacate the emotional, psychological premises; that girls tangle endlessly with their moms and that dads have the sex talk with their sons and check out from their daughters' lives. Of course, we all know that these are simplistic reductions. It takes a lot of courage to come to terms with the truth that our children are now sexual, almost as much as it takes for kids to do the same, and for the same reasons. And it takes a lot of love and time to remain committed to our children as they change in ways that are upsetting and exhilarating at the same time.

Still, the onset of puberty means that adolescence is brewing in the near distance. This is a time when parents are suddenly no longer the center of their kids' lives—or so it may seem. Instead of looking up at you when you talk, they look down on you for holding your old views. Instead of wanting to keep company with you on the way to the store, they scrunch down in their seat when they drive by their friends. But do not allow their demeanor to deceive you. You still matter more than they will ever say in their suddenly cracking voices. Everything you have done throughout childhood is an investment in the future. This is when they need you to move slightly to the side, to wait for their cues and questions and concerns to emerge and guide you. It is a time, therefore, of maximum vulnerability for everybody, a time when mutual trust will reward both you and your growing children.

eleven

The Shadow of the Internet

How Does Sexual Curiosity Relate to My Child's Integrity?

Contemporary youth detect the profound cynicism that permeates our society but wish for more honesty, compassion, responsibility, and loyalty.

—Jerome Kagan, *Three Seductive Ideas*

When my love swears that she is made of truth,
I do believe her, though I know she lies.

—William Shakespeare, Sonnet 138

THE BIRDS AND THE BYTES

—One—

It was early in the morning, and Kathy still hadn't left for work. Her son, Scott, was accomplished in the art of stalling, and today he was in top form. Ever since he had begun middle school, Kathy and Beth had noticed an escalation in his delaying tactics. But it was different from when he was four. Then he got sidetracked by everything, or he lingered to get his two moms' attention. Now it was if he could not wake up; he went from task to task like a sleepwalker. He was already twelve, and they wondered if these signals were road signs to puberty.

Scott was sweet and innocent, Kathy reassured herself: He loved cuddling between the two of them while watching a movie; he was proud of them when they came to his games (which was most of the time); he liked sitting between them at church. But then again, watching him lumber out the door with Beth, late for school again, brought back Kathy's anxiety over Scott's impending adolescence. So far they had handled everything without a hitch: balancing their work schedules so one of them was always home to meet him, helping him field the questions about his two moms and the whereabouts of his dad, and supporting him through a difficult transition into middle school.

Scott wasn't an extrovert, and he was having difficulty dealing with all the new faces at school as well as with a schedule that had him moving from room to room and teacher to teacher all day. This was a tricky transition for most kids, but especially for Scott, as he had come from an elementary school where he had been with the same kids in the same room with the same teachers for years. Near the end of last year, however, the teachers had advised Kathy and Beth to expect some bumpiness when he entered public middle school but that within a few months he would flourish.

As Kathy made one last run through the house, she checked—for the second time—that the oven was off, the coffee machine unplugged, and the backdoor dead-bolted. Beth called her obsessive, but then again, it wouldn't kill Beth to be a bit more meticulous herself. As she walked down the hall, glancing in rooms for preventable disasters, she heard Scott's computer announce that he had e-mail. Kathy wondered how many more times she would have to tell Scott to turn off his computer. She hated the idea of wasting all that electricity.

She sat down at Scott's computer, dumped the screen saver, and prepared to log off. She closed his e-mail account, got off-line, and then began to close his programs, one by one—the word processor, a drawing program, some new video game, and finally she came to his web browser. She hesitated. Then, for some reason she would never understand, she hit the History button on Scott's web browser.

If she had any doubts before she hit that button, they vanished. Puberty was upon Scott, and upon Kathy and Beth by association. There, staring out from her son's computer screen, was a list of what looked to be porn sites: free and sex and hot and babes, all dot-com.

"My little boy," she mused.

–Two–

Later that morning, as Kathy sat down at the kitchen counter with the phone to her ear, waiting for Beth to pick up her call, she marveled at all that was about to happen.

"Our day has arrived," said Kathy.

"I've only got a couple of minutes before this meeting. What's up?"

"Are you sitting down? I'm not kidding, Beth, are you sitting yet?"

"Is Scott OK?"

"Oh, Scott is fine. Very healthy in fact. Maybe too healthy."

Beth knew Kathy wouldn't tell her what was going on until she sounded under control. It wasn't worth a fight, so she took a few seconds to quiet herself. "OK, Ms. Control Freak. I'm sitting down and my door is closed."

"It's official, our twelve-year-old son has hit puberty."

"Did he receive a merit badge in the mail?"

"Just about," she said. She told her what she had found on Scott's computer.

All Beth could think to do was breathe.

—Three—

That afternoon, when Scott got home from school, both his parents were waiting for him. Something was up, he could sense, and whatever it was, it wasn't good. After school it was one or the other, Beth or Kathy, but never both.

Beth tried, maybe too hard, to sound casual. "How was school?"

"What's wrong?"

"I'm just wondering how your day was, that's all."

"Then why are both of you here?"

It was Kathy's turn. "We need to talk with you about something."

"I'm not going to like this, am I?"

This time they answered together. "Probably not." And then they all headed toward the dining-room table, where their big talks took place.

Beth started. "Scott, you left your computer on this morning, again."

Scott shifted forward in his chair and leaned both elbows on the table. "This is all because I left my computer on? All right, I'll make sure I don't do it again. Can I go now?"

"Not so fast. We're not meeting because you left your computer on but because of what was on your computer."

"You searched my computer?"

Beth jumped in. "No, we didn't search your computer. Not at first, anyway. But when you leave it on, someone has to turn it off. And when Kathy was closing down the machine, she found something that disturbs us both."

"I can't believe you're spying on me."

Kathy took this one. "I wasn't spying, not really. I just hit the History button on your web browser, which we told you we would do from time to time when we got you your on-line account. Remember?"

It took a few seconds, but soon Scott recalled what Kathy had probably discovered on his web browser. "So?"

"So, I found a bunch of porno sites."

"Those aren't mine."

"What do you mean," said Beth, "they aren't yours?"

"Don't you believe me?"

Kathy jumped in. "If they're not yours, then how did they get there?"

They both saw a flash of humiliation streak across Scott's face, then a surge of tears.

Beth handed Scott some tissues, and they waited.

"Jason and Elvin showed me those web sites the other day at school."

"You were searching for porn sites at school?" asked Beth. "How did you have time at school to look for porn sites?"

"At lunch, in the computer room. There's hardly ever anybody there. Elvin was into it. Then he dared Jason and me. It's not like it was my idea, but I couldn't back down, either."

"Why not?"

"We dare each other all the time. We get bored."

"You did this on a dare? How can you be bored?" Kathy wanted to know. "You're twelve years old. Never mind, let's stay on your computer. How did those sites get on your computer?"

"We put all the URLs in an e-mail that we sent to all of us, a couple of other friends, too. So when I saw the e-mail last night, I opened it and went to some of the sites."

"So you did look at them?"

"I wasn't trying to. I just got carried away. It's not like I surfed for them myself."

"But now you're looking at them on your own, in your bedroom. So something's changed," Kathy suggested.

"Not really, I told you, we did it at school. And only because Elvin dared me."

"I'm having trouble following your logic, Scott," said Kathy.

"Mom. Everybody does it; it's normal."

"That means if everybody—"

"Jumps off a cliff? No, that doesn't mean I would jump, too."

"Well, looks like you just did," said Beth.

"Scott, there's nothing wrong with exploring your sexuality," Kathy said. "In fact, it's an important part of who we are. But pornography is a different matter, and that's what has us so upset right now. We told you when we got you your computer that we didn't want you to surf for pornography."

"I'm not following *your* logic. You're telling me sex is OK but I can't look at those web sites?"

"Good question. And yes, it's what we're saying, because there is a difference between pornography and sexuality."

Scott looked at them as if they were out of their minds. And his parents recognized that look. Could he have a point?

"This is a great place to take a break," said Kathy, standing up. "But in the meantime, we won't tolerate your surfing the web for pornography. So stay off-line until we can talk again, probably to-morrow."

"Can I check my e-mail?"

"No, not yet."

"That's so unfair."

"We can see why you think so, but that's the way it is. Now let's clear the table for dinner."

NOTES HOME

Pornography challenges every parent's integrity, as well as every child's. And it challenges us even if we are the most ardent sup-porters of the First Amendment. This kind of event can take place in any sort of family and in any community in the world. That's re-ality. This does not mean that parents should throw up their hands. Although Scott's parents may have formed a nontraditional family, there is nothing more conventional and predictable than a boy's interest in sex and pornography. But the exploration of pornography is only one piece of the puzzle of Scott's development. Just as important are Scott's relationships with his friends and his parents.

A Parent's Rude Awakening

All parents are disappointed when moments like this occur. But what are we disappointed about? Are we afraid we have let our children down? Or that they have let us down? And when we consider our distress and the stakes involved for our kids, is there a difference?

Still, it takes commitment and patience to sort through these questions and struggle through this experience, as Kathy and Beth are finding out. Their challenge now is to turn the family conversation eventually into one about love, relationship, and trust. And they must, at some point, articulate this goal. Their purpose cannot be to simply get pornography out of the house and out of Scott's life. Certainly, without question, that's important to do. But before they can effectively do so, they must understand what Scott is going through and act upon what he needs from them—boundaries, information, empathy, and pragmatic guidance. Above all else, they shouldn't take Scott's behavior personally. It's not about them, it's about Scott's growing up. If they need to blame anybody, we nominate Charles Darwin.

Although it may seem strange, Kathy and Beth ought to be thankful that they caught Scott. If they had "covered" pornography and sexuality before Scott reached puberty (as they seem to have done), it's likely Scott heard only about a third of what they were saying. At that time, the information would not have seemed germane to his life. Now, after this incident, they can be sure they have his full attention. This is not to say it was a bad idea to cover this material ahead of time; in fact, all their groundwork is going to help them through the current crisis. And though it is not life and

death, this is a crisis. Bottom line: What they say and do now rein-
forces what they said and did before, building on it when Scott
most needs it, as he crashes into puberty. So now, more than ever,
what they have to say can make a difference to Scott. Whether his
parents realize it or not, they've been preparing for difficult conversations like this since Scott was born. As their children approach
adolescence, parents should prepare to revisit most of their previous big conversations: sex, alcohol, cigarettes, drugs, cheating. Parenting is recursive.

So, what's on the dining-room table for Kathy and Beth? Plenty.

- Keeping pornography out of the house
- Encouraging Scott to understand the implications of what he
  has done
- Forging a connection between Scott's behavior and his in-
  tegrity
- Helping Scott see the effects of peer pressure
- Fostering trust in their child
- Affirming sexuality and the value of exploration
- Making clear what Scott should expect of himself
- Showing Scott that they love him
- Keeping the lines of communication open

Spying?

Did Scott want to be found out? He would deny it, probably. But he
is the one who left the computer on with a slightly obsessive mom
who checks and rechecks everything before she leaves the house. It
is a good bet, therefore, that he is indicating through his actions
that he needs help and support.

Staring at the looming mushroom cloud of adolescence, some
parents feel desperate enough to search their children's rooms and
backpacks, to go through their diaries and e-mails, and to eaves-

drop on their phone conversations. This strategy is destined to backfire. Of course, it is one thing to be proactive when it comes to a child who has had problems. Perhaps a child who has been discovered smoking cigarettes provides justification to go through the garbage or look inside dresser drawers. Two provisos here: (1) The search warrant has a time limit and need only be in effect until trust is earned back; and (2) you need to explain to your child the terms and purpose of the warrant. If you do not, it will feel like a violation, not only of your child's room but also of your relationship with your child.

But the child who has not previously given cause for concern should be given the benefit of the doubt, and privacy. The last thing we want to do is violate the integrity of our relationship with our children. When they get older and routinely face difficult choices, your having trusted them when they deserved to be trusted will give them the capability to trust themselves to do the right thing. Once again, integrity begets integrity.

Sexual Awareness and Masturbation

One of the realities of puberty is masturbation. Some parents might find masturbation objectionable on moral grounds. Other parents encourage their children to explore their bodies on their own. Most psychologists and sex educators regard masturbation as indispensable to the development of healthy sexuality. These clinicians and teachers believe that masturbation permits people to get to know what feels good, what feels bad, and everything in between. In part, this notion relates to future mutual relationships, when individuals can prompt their partners on what excites and pleases them.

In other words, there is plenty of diverse opinion on the topic. Parents can be understandably unnerved when they contemplate what their kids do by themselves behind closed doors, but the truth is that "masturbation does not cause any kind of physical harm . . . The main problems associated with masturbation are psychological: the guilt and anxiety some people feel who masturbate."[1] We all know there is much more to sexuality than just the physical side. As parents, you need to make sure your kids understand their bodies, and you need to explain your stance as to the moral and psychological ramifications of their sexual behaviors. If Scott's parents threw the sex ed book on the bed, they could reasonably assume he would skip the introduction.

As for masturbation, we believe that your child's curiosity is a force that neither the child nor you can ignore. As Michael Gurian, author of *A Fine Young Man*, says: "A boy's interest in masturbation is in self-care, in quick physical tension release, in the new kind of power the body possesses—in many things that need, for the sake of the boy and his healthy journey, to be fully understood and, finally, enjoyed."[2] Girls masturbate for similar reasons: self-discovery, pleasure, and independence.

Wherever you stand on the spectrum of views, you still need to talk with your children about their emerging sexuality when puberty is knocking on the door. For pubescent children, masturbation brings a host of complications not experienced by previous generations, not the least of which relates to the Internet. As sexuality develops in children these days, they will look for information and sources in a place that is natural to them—the Internet. But the Internet, as we all know, is not innocent.

Boys and Girls on the Internet

In terms of sexual stimulation, males tend to be more visual than females. Before the Internet, pubescent boys might have searched for a worn, torn copy of *Playboy*. The Internet has made the *Playboy* rite of passage irrelevant, obsolete, and downright quaint. Now, all a boy has to do is open a web browser and type in almost any sexual word and he will get an astounding number of sites more than ready to satisfy his curiosity. Sure, parents can load filtering software that makes it much more difficult for children to access these sites on their home computers, but no filtering device is foolproof. Software only makes the effort more difficult, not impossible. As soon as you construct a barrier, your kids (and the porn purveyors) use their ingenuity to get around it. What's more, if your son cannot access a site on the home computer, he can usually access it on a friend's or on the one at the local library.

For girls, and remember we are speaking of course in sweeping stereotypes, sexual excitement proceeds from relationship as well as visual stimulation. Females tend to need conversation and connection. In terms of the Internet, then, the site of girls' explorations and sexual interest is usually not a pornographic web address, but chat rooms, where fantasy relationships are shaped. Ominously, this is the place where evil can lurk behind the masks of cybernames: "Stevie," the supposed sixteen-year-old athlete and honor-roll student, may actually be "Stefan," the forty-three-year-old sex offender. And the danger of such "encounters" may be more difficult to get across to our daughters than the more or less obvious degradations of pornography.

An important recent study will not allay our fears. According to researchers, 20 percent of children who go on-line are solicited for sex. "And neither the presence of Internet filters nor parental monitoring of children's Internet use decreased the likelihood that a child would be sexually solicited by a stranger online."[3] The millions of middle schoolers who go on-line every day need to be told that they can and should reach out to parents and other adults. *If you ever get a message inviting you into a private chat room or asking for your name or phone number, leave the computer on and find me. And if you can't find me, call the police. If you don't turn the computer off, they can trace the messages. This is serious and we won't be mad at you. Just the opposite. We'll be proud because it means we can trust you to ask for help when you're in over your head.*

Sad to say, there is nothing you can do to guarantee that your child will never explore the world of Internet pornography or on-line "relationships." Guardian software and usage guidelines, while necessary, skirt the overarching issue. Again, clarity comes through the lens of integrity, by focusing on that part of your children that realizes something is amiss in the conversation they are having with sixteen-year-old "Stevie" or in the images that they are seeing on their screens.

Now is the time to explain, or reaffirm, your views on pornography, sexuality, childhood, and the like. Even if you think pornography is an acceptable adult interest, for children, at this formative stage of their development, it jeopardizes their integrity in at least the following ways:

- Pornography degrades the observer.
- Pornography commercially exploits people.
- Pornography desensitizes viewers.
- Pornography skews perceptions of relationships and sexuality.
- Pornography objectifies human beings and commodifies intimacy.

Before you can forge the connection between integrity and behavior, you need to investigate why it is that your daughter seeks out such connection in cyberspace or why your son desires the stimulation of cyberpornography. For most girls who find themselves in this situation, it is a function of need and timing. She is feeling alienated from her friends when she first enters a chat room, whereupon she meets "Stevie," who seems to know her better than she knows herself. Now she chooses to pursue this new and exciting "relationship." On-line, she can also explore parts of herself that she feels are repressed in her everyday life. In addition, she neglects the painful, more vulnerable work of reconfiguring her real-life relationships in favor of seeking unconditional acceptance offered by somebody who does not know her at all.

Similarly, for boys, it is again a matter of need and timing. He is anxious and overwhelmed by his increasingly complex life: friends who are changing, academics that are more stressful, and athletics whose demands exceed his skill. Giving over to this anxiety, he visits a porn site and discovers that the intoxication of this type of sexual stimulation permits him escape for a minute. (This dynamic is just as true for kids who get hooked into games over the Internet.) But of course, most boys who surf the net do so for marathon sessions, and this compulsivity is a clue for us to track down. What we will discover is that it is not an escape to the pictures as much as it is an escape from their loneliness. Every minute spent surfing on-line is a minute away from his troubles and his isolation. This, not the sordid images, is the issue parents should be most concerned about.

THE NEXT CONVERSATION

The next evening, Beth and Kathy had reorganized their thoughts sufficiently to have the follow-up integrity talk. They thought it best to not overwhelm Scott by teaming up on him. Beth lost the coin toss, so she spoke with Scott alone.

—Scott, can we talk some more?

—About getting back my e-mail?

—Not yet. We still have some other stuff to figure out.

—I told you already that I'm not into that stuff.

—Well, to us that's not really clear.

—This isn't the birds and the bees, is it? I still haven't finished that book you left on my bed.

—Not really. Well, sort of, I guess. Actually it's a much more important conversation. You broke your word and lied to us. That hurt.

—I didn't lie to you. I told you where I got those web sites.

—No, Scott, this is bigger than just telling the truth, and it's as much about the future as it is about what happened yesterday. I know this will be difficult for both of us, but I need to ask. When you were looking at those pornographic web sites, what kinds of thoughts were going on in your mind?

—You're kidding, right?

—OK, fair enough. How about afterwards?

—I don't know. I thought it was kind of stupid. It all looked so fake.

—What else? Did you feel good about yourself? Bad? A mix of good and bad?

—It felt a little weird. I didn't like it, but I couldn't stop, either.

—What was it you didn't like?

—I didn't like the way it made me feel. That it wasn't right somehow to look at those pictures.

—How wasn't it right?

—I don't know. It just felt bad, sort of dirty. I know it was wrong to do, but it felt more than just wrong, just not right somehow.

—Do you know what part of you was feeling and thinking that way?

—No, not really.

—That was what Kathy and I have talked about with you before. It was your integrity talking.

—I guess.

—So if you had listened to that part of yourself when you got those e-mails, what might you have done differently? What advice was it giving you?

—I don't think I would have done anything different. It wasn't until I opened the sites that I began to feel bad.

—OK, Scott, this is not about making you feel any worse. Though I'm glad you feel bad. This is about how you learn from your mistakes.

—You said masturbation was OK.

—It's a good thing to find out about your feelings and your body, but it's not a good thing to lie to us and it's not a good thing to let your imagination get caught up in these images. And I'll prove to you, right now, that you know exactly what I'm talking about. If it was a good thing, you wouldn't have lied to us.

Meeting Kids at Eye Level

Counselors are taught to ask open-ended questions when they talk to others in a supportive manner: *How do you feel about that? Why did you respond like that? What was that like for you?* With adults, these are expansive, probing, productive questions. When friends ask you one of these questions, it indicates they are curious about what you have to say. And in response, you can find yourself saying and feeling things that never occurred to you before. With children, however, these same kinds of questions are met with confused stares. This is because starting the conversation off with open-ended questions can be overwhelming to most kids, so parents are wise to take a slightly more indirect approach.

With children, parents are always more successful when they tie these more open-ended questions to specific examples, as Beth did: *What were you thinking when you were looking at those pornographic web sites? . . . Anyway, as you looked at those sites, what were you feeling? . . . Glad to hear that, Scott. Do you know what part of you was feeling and thinking that way? . . . Did you feel good about yourself? . . . Bad? . . . A mix of good and bad? . . . How wasn't it right? . . .* These are all examples of concrete questions tied to specific content. Afterward, a parent can ask the open-ended questions and stand a much better chance of success. That is, the pieces are all lined up to be put together in a coherent, global understanding of the event. It just takes patience and persistence to get there.

Now What?

Beth and Kathy have been respectful in their treatment of Scott, while voicing their views on pornography as well as reasserting the values at play in their home. But there is much to do, now that the philosophical issues have been addressed. Parents who are mortified and self-conscious of their embarrassment—parents who send the message simply to behave or obey—are consistently going to find themselves out of the loop. Their children will find it difficult to trust them with complex problems.

So how can parents help their children? Let's be pragmatic.

Recognizing that Scott is on the brink of puberty, and that he has friends already there, his parents have the opportunity to support his integrity through some simple interventions. Where, for instance, should Scott's computer be situated in the near future? It is better to remove temptation from a pubescent boy than to try and force him to summon up the necessary willpower to resist. A little bit of anticipation goes a long way in creating character. Beth and Kathy need to consider either removing the computer from Scott's room or limiting his Internet access, and this is not done as punishment but as support. That is, he has enough going on in his life without having to conjure up the strength to resist the lure of the sexual explicitness only a click away on his computer. Instead, his parents simplify his life. Now when he next sees his friends, his parents have become the bad guys: "Hey, don't send me anymore of those web site addresses. My parents pulled my computer and put it in the living room, alongside theirs. It's a drag, but if they catch me going to those sites, all hell will break loose, and it isn't worth it."

Speaking of Jason and Elvin, Beth and Kathy may well consider communicating with their parents. It is what they would appreciate, after all, if the shoe were on the other foot. But the integrity of Scott's parents comes into play here, too. They need to be careful not to blame his friends. And they need to be clear that all they are doing is giving other parents the information that they will find useful in raising their own children.

There is one other issue to address as well: the dare. Smart kids, good kids, are dared to ride their bike on a retaining wall, to play with firecrackers, to shoplift, and, yes, to view forbidden materials. Unfortunately, most of us learn about the stupidity of accepting a dare the hard way—we fall off the wall, burn our fingertips, get caught. A dare is seductive. In taking a dare, we feel powerful, courageous, and singled out. *No one else will do this. I will.* In kid-speak, that's tough to argue with. Our children will dare others and be dared themselves. But when their integrity is important to them, they will recognize the folly and futility of doing anything to impress somebody else or to live up to an inauthentic and reckless image of themselves.

Being Twelve: The Age of For and Against

Being twelve means being one small step away from being a teenager. Twelve-year-olds are more secure and independent than they were at eleven. They are more candid in their assessment of their limitations and failings. They are full of energy, and their sexual curiosity is peaking. They are articulate to the point of being outspoken. And most poignantly, they are a little bit worried about where they are going. It's a time of great excitement and risk. "Just Say No" is a thing of the past. They will try to be open-minded about smoking, drugs, alcohol, and sex. There will be opportunities to experiment. In other words, they will make some mistakes that will shock you. Now, instead of finding your shoes under their bed, you may find a pack of cigarettes. When you tell them it is time for sleep, they may ignore you and sneak a little more television.

Twelve is a time of conflict. But it is not all bleakness and warfare—for as much as they want to define themselves by resisting you, twelve-year-olds will also yearn to maintain their connection with you. Even though they are pushing you a bit to the side, you are still central to their existence and well-being, which is why you have conflict in the first place.

The Last Word

Scott and his parents have some tough times on the horizon. Eventually, though not too soon, they can all take the high road, where the horizon seems to rise up to meet them. There will arrive an opportunity for all of them to underscore what they have been through and where they are going. Scott is on his way to full-blown adolescence and adulthood. If his parents find a way to emphasize how much they love him, how normal his experience has been, and that they forgive him, then they can feel a little bit more confident about Scott's forming real-life connections with living, breathing people. Isn't puberty, ultimately, a portal to love?

Afterword

The Needle of the Compass

A child said *What is the grass?* fetching it to me with full hands;
How could I answer the child? I do not know what it is any more
than he.

—Walt Whitman, *Song of Myself*

One day, and probably when we least expect it, childhood comes to an end. It is strange that we never expected it, yet it is still somehow unthinkable. Our children suddenly put on an article of clothing we never saw before. They announce a dietary revolt. They ask us to call them by another name. The fight goes on way too long. And we can't figure out what we are fighting about. Or perhaps the fight never starts. Music pours from behind the closed door of their room and leaves us covering up our ears. They take up religion or politics or art in a new way—or drop them suddenly with a thud.

Before we know it, however, another feeling will kick in. We are not completely letting go at all. We are always there, available, off to the side, ready for them to reach out. The loss of one kind of relationship with our rapidly growing children will be filled by a very different kind of relationship with that new human being who is now our teenager. The experience is hardly that clear-cut, of course, and there will be lots of opportunities to observe surges of growth as well as slides of regression. Although we will hear others say different, the truth is that emerging adolescence can be an exhilarating time, as long as we keep the long view. In the short term, our kids change so quickly and right before our eyes that we keep blinking and shaking our heads, not sure if we are hallucinating.

We will have an accurate sense of childhood's end when we realize that any external incentives (punishments as well as rewards) are not working as well as they once did. Those time-outs that did wonders when children were seven suddenly seem beside the point, if not downright unworkable.

Along about this time, however, we will see the effect of having instilled integrity all along. Yes, in a sense, we may well feel radically powerless. But then comes the recognition: There is power in that powerlessness. For now, equipped with their sense of personal integrity, our children are becoming more and more capable of leading their own lives. Once we were their encyclopedia. Now we are their hyperlink. Once we were their protector. Now we are an adviser, an advocate, a mirror, a sounding board, a consultant.

Remember that day when we removed the training wheels from the gleaming bicycle—and we held our breath, or crossed our fingers, or prayed? Recall how our child fell off that bike for the first time? Keep that memory alive. There are lessons to cherish in it. We dusted them off, applied the healing, multicolored bandages, rubbed their heads, and helped them back up. Sometimes they fell off yet again, sometimes they made it all the way to the corner. Somehow, throughout their growing up, it will continue to be like that, in a way. They will continue to fall off bikes from time to time as they grow up. Only these bikes will have other names: academics, athletics, romance, and so on. Yes, the stakes are higher. A car is nothing like a bike. And not getting off the bench and into a Little League game is not quite like not getting into the college of their dreams. Yet they survived those disappointments and defeats, and with luck and our steadying love, they will survive these, too.

So, here we are. What awaits us? And what awaits them? Our imagination leads us to summon up some crucibles for both of us: Going to parties. Driving. Falling in love. Facing academic and intellectual challenges. Forging lifelong friendships. Enduring peer pressures. Experiencing sexuality. Taking risks. Seeking their passions—the arts, athletics, community service, leadership, work. Going to the prom (or not). Dating (or not). Applying to college (or not). Moving one day away from home (or not).

Every single day, our children undergo a potentially formative experience. And it is formative only because we *form* the connection between their experience and their integrity. If we do this early on, then most of our conversations during adolescence will have a reference point as steady as an anchor. Our focus will not be to control our teenagers but to get them to listen to the voice within. *"What stopped you from listening to that part of you that knew the right thing to do?"*

For the truth may be the truth, and a falsehood, a falsehood, but even the Golden Rule (Treat others as you would like to be treated) and the Ten Commandments admit to gray areas when applied to our actual day-to-day lives. If in our grappling with a hard choice we do not see a gray area, then we are probably not looking and imagining hard enough. In fact, if there were not gray areas, there would have been no need for the Ten Commandments in the first place; it would have been obvious. Rules, even the Golden Rule, are the starting points of conversation and thinking, not the final solution.

We are not being relativistic when we say this, either. Moral relativists apparently believe that all moral choices are equivalent or arbitrary. Maybe we have never actually met a moral relativist, because we believe that for all of us in the destined so-called moment of truth, and in relationship with others, certain moral choices are better, fairer, and more honest than others. Our children can embrace their integrity, and it will sustain them. It just isn't easy. Harder than anything else, though, is living without it.

Augustine of Hippo (354–430), also known as Saint Augustine, wrote one of the greatest, most unflinching autobiographies, a book continually mined for insight into childhood and growth by psychologists and historians and readers of literature. It was Augustine who slyly said, "Love God and do whatever you want." We would secularize and adapt his wisdom for our purposes: "Be in integrity and do whatever you want." This is the most solid peg in the world upon which to hang our hat—for without it, our children cannot know who they are and where they are going. And with the compass of their own integrity, they can go anywhere with a clear conscience. Isn't that what we will always hope for them?

NOTES

Introduction

1. Stephen L. Carter, *Integrity* (New York: Harper, 1997), 7.
2. Tim O'Brien, *The Things They Carried* (Boston: Houghton Mifflin/Seymour Lawrence, 1990), 166.

Chapter 1

1. For an excellent discussion of being five years old, see Louise Bates Ames and Frances L. Ilg, *Your Five-Year-Old* (New York: Dell, 1979).

Chapter 2

1. Malcolm Gladwell, *The Tipping Point* (New York: Little, Brown, 2000), 105–106.
2. For an excellent discussion of being six years old, see Louise Bates Ames and Frances L. Ilg, *Your Six-Year-Old* (New York: Dell, 1979).
3. Bruno Bettelheim, *A Good Enough Parent* (New York: Vintage, 1987), 366–367.

Chapter 3

1. For an excellent discussion of being seven years old, see Louise Bates Ames and Carol Chase Haber, *Your Seven-Year-Old* (New York: Dell, 1985).
2. Thomas Lewis, Fari Amini, and Richard Lannon, *A General Theory of Love* (New York: Vintage, 2000), 79.

Chapter 4

1. Mark Twain Papers, Notebook 35, May–October 1895, Bancroft Library, University of California, Berkeley.

Chapter 5

1. For an excellent discussion of being eight years old, see Louise Bates Ames and Carol Chase Haber, *Your Eight-Year-Old* (New York: Dell, 1989).

Chapter 9

1. Jim Thompson, "If Winning Is the Only Thing, Kids Lose," *San Francisco Chronicle*, July 8, 2001.

Chapter 10

1. Jane E. Brody, "Yesterday's Precocious Puberty Is Norm Today," *New York Times*, November 30, 1999.

2. Lisa Collier Cool, "The Secret Sex Life of Kids," *Ladies' Home Journal* (March 2001):157.

Chapter 11

1. June M. Reinisch, with Ruth Beasley, *The Kinsey Institute New Report on Sex* (New York: St. Martin's Press, 1991), 95.

2. Michael Gurian, *A Fine Young Man* (New York: Tarcher/Putnam, 1998), 93.

3. John Schwartz, "Studies Detail Solicitation of Children for Sex Online," *New York Times*, June 20, 2001.

BIBLIOGRAPHY

Ahrons, Constance. *The Good Divorce: Keeping Your Family Together When Your Marriage Comes Apart.* New York: HarperPerennial, 1994.

Ames, Louise Bates, and Carol Chase Haber. *Your Seven-Year-Old: Life in a Minor Key.* New York: Dell, 1985.

_____. *Your Eight-Year-Old: Lively and Outgoing.* New York: Dell, 1989.

_____. *Your Nine-Year-Old: Thoughtful and Mysterious.* New York: Dell, 1990.

Ames, Louise Bates, and Frances L. Ilg. *Your Five-Year-Old: Sunny and Serene.* New York: Dell, 1979.

_____. *Your Six-Year-Old: Loving and Defiant.* New York: Dell, 1979.

Ames, Louise Bates, Frances L. Ilg, and Sidney M. Barker. *Your Ten- to Fourteen-Year-Old.* New York: Dell, 1988.

Banner, James M., and Harold C. Cannon. *The Elements of Teaching.* New Haven, CT: Yale University Press, 1997.

Bell, Ruth. *Changing Bodies, Changing Lives: A Book for Teens on Sex and Relationships.* 3rd ed. New York: Times Books, 1998.

Belle, Deborah. *The After-School Lives of Children: Alone and with Others While Parents Work.* Mahwah, NJ: Lawrence Erlbaum Associates, 1999.

Berger, Elizabeth. *Raising Children with Character: Parents, Trust, and the Development of Personal Integrity.* Northvale, NJ: Jason Aronson, 1999.

Bettelheim, Bruno. *A Good Enough Parent: A Book on Child-Rearing.* New York: Vintage, 1987.

Borba, Michele. *Building Moral Intelligence: The Seven Essential Virtues That Teach Kids to Do the Right Thing.* San Francisco: Jossey-Bass, 2001.

Brazelton, T. Berry. *Touchpoints: Your Child's Emotional and Behavioral Development.* Boston: Perseus, 1994.

Brumberg, Joan Jacobs. *The Body Project: An Intimate History of American Girls.* New York: Random House, 1997.

Campbell, Jeremy. *The Liar's Tale: A History of Falsehood*. New York: Norton, 2001.

Carter, Stephen L. *Integrity*. New York: Harper, 1997.

Dreikurs, Rudolf. *Children: The Challenge*. New York: Hawthorn/Dutton, 1964.

Erikson, Erik. *Childhood and Society*. New York: Norton, 1963.

_____. *Identity: Youth and Crisis*. New York: Norton, 1968.

Faber, Adele, and Elaine Mazlish. *How to Talk So Kids Will Listen and Listen So Kids Will Talk*. New York: Avon Books, 1980.

Fass, Paula S., and Mary Ann Mason. *Childhood in America*. New York: New York University Press, 2000.

Fraiberg, Selma H. *The Magic Years: Understanding and Handling the Problems of Early Childhood*. New York: Simon and Schuster, 1959.

Frankl, Viktor E. *Man's Search for Meaning: An Introduction to Logotherapy*. New York: Touchstone, 1984.

Galinsky, Ellen. *Ask the Children: What America's Children Really Think About Working Parents*. New York: William Morrow and Company, 1999.

Gardner, Howard. *Multiple Intelligences: The Theory in Practice*. New York: Basic, 1993.

Gilligan, Carol. *In a Different Voice*. Cambridge, MA: Harvard University Press, 1982.

Gladwell, Malcolm. *The Tipping Point: How Little Things Can Make a Big Difference*. New York: Little, Brown and Company, 2000.

Goleman, Daniel. *Emotional Intelligence*. New York: Bantam Books, 1995.

Gurian, Michael. *A Fine Young Man: What Parents, Mentors, and Educators Can Do to Shape Adolescent Boys into Exceptional Men*. New York: Tarcher/Putnam, 1998.

_____. *The Good Son: Shaping the Moral Development of Our Boys and Young Men*. New York: Tarcher/Putnam, 1999.

Hallowell, Edward M., and John J. Ratey. *Driven to Distraction: Recognizing and Coping with Attention Deficit Disorder from Childhood Through Adulthood*. New York: Simon and Schuster, 1994.

Inaba, Darryl S., and William E. Cohen. *Uppers, Downers, and All Arounders*. Ashland, OR: CNS Productions, 1983.

Jalloun, Tahar Ben. *Racism Explained to My Daughter*. New York: New Press, 1999.

Kabat-Zinn, Myla, and Jon Kabat-Zinn. *Everyday Blessings: The Inner Work of Mindful Parenting*. New York: Hyperion, 1997.

Kegan, Robert. *The Evolving Self: Problem and Process in Human Development.* Cambridge, MA: Harvard University Press, 1982.

Kelly, Gary F. *Learning About Sex: The Contemporary Guide for Young Adults.* 3rd ed. New York: Barron's Educational Series, 1987.

Kindlon, Dan, and Michael Thompson. *Raising Cain: Protecting the Emotional Life of Boys.* New York: Ballantine, 1999.

Kohn, Alfie. *Punished by Rewards.* New York: Houghton Mifflin, 1995.

Kübler-Ross, Elisabeth. *Death: The Final Stage of Growth.* Englewood Cliffs, NJ: Prentice-Hall, 1975.

Lerner, Harriet. *The Mother Dance: How Children Change Your Life.* New York: HarperPerennial, 1998.

Levine, Mel. *Developmental Variation and Learning Disorders.* Cambridge, MA: Educational Publishing Service, 1983.

_____. *Educational Care: A System for Understanding and Helping Children with Learning Problems at Home and in School.* Cambridge, MA: Educational Publishing Service, 1994.

Lewis, Thomas, Fari Amini, and Richard Lannon. *A General Theory of Love.* New York: Vintage Books, 2000.

Maderas, Lynda, Dane Saavedra, and Ralph Lopez. *What's Happening to My Body? Book for Boys: A Growing Up Guide for Parents and Sons.* New York: Newmarket, 1987.

Maderas, Lynda, Claudia Ziroli, and Jackie Aher. *What's Happening to My Body? Book for Girls: A Growing Up Guide for Parents and Daughters.* New York: Newmarket, 1987.

Montessori, Maria. *The Absorbent Mind.* New York: Henry Holt, 1967.

Moore, Thomas. *Care of the Soul: A Guide for Cultivating Depth and Sacredness in Everyday Life.* New York: HarperPerennial, 1992.

Newberger, Eli H. *The Men They Will Become: The Nature and Nurture of Male Character.* Reading, MA: Perseus, 1999.

Parent, Marc. *Believing It All: What My Children Taught Me About Trout Fishing, Jelly Toast, and Life.* New York: Little, Brown, 2001.

Pipher, Mary. *Reviving Ophelia: Saving the Selves of Adolescent Girls.* New York: Putnam, 1994.

Pollack, William. *Real Boys: Rescuing Our Sons from the Myths of Boyhood.* New York: Random House, 1998.

Reinisch, June M., with Ruth Beasley. *The Kinsey Institute New Report on Sex.* New York: St. Martin's Press, 1991.

Riera, Michael. *Surviving High School.* Berkeley, CA: Celestial Arts, 1997.

_____. *Uncommon Sense for Parents with Teenagers*. Berkeley, CA: Celestial Arts, 1995.

Riera, Michael, and Joseph Di Prisco. *Field Guide to the American Teenager*. Cambridge, MA: Perseus Publishing, 2000.

Rimm, Sylvia. *See Jane Win*. New York: Three Rivers Press, 1999.

Roffman, Deborah. *Sex and Sensibility: A Parent's Guide to Talking About Sex*. Cambridge, MA: Perseus Publishing, 2001.

Rubin, Zick. *Children's Friendships: The Developing Child*. Cambridge, MA: Harvard University Press, 1980.

Rutter, Virginia Beane. *Embracing Persephone: How to Be the Mother You Want for the Daughter You Cherish*. New York: Kodansha International, 2000.

Ryan, Joan. *Little Girls in Pretty Boxes: The Making and Breaking of Elite Gymnasts and Figure Skaters*. New York: Warner, 1995.

Schank, Roger. *Coloring Outside the Lines*. New York: HarperCollins Publishers, 2000.

Schor, Edward L., ed. *Caring for Your School-Age Child: Ages 5 to 12*. Rev. ed. New York: Bantam, 1999.

Schwartz, Pepper, and Dominic Cappello. *Ten Talks Parents Must Have with Their Children About Sex and Character*. New York: Hyperion, 2000.

Severe, Sal. *How to Behave So Your Children Will, Too*. New York: Viking, 2000.

Shandler, Sara. *Ophelia Speaks: Adolescent Girls Write About Their Search for Self*. New York: Harper, 1999.

Smaldino, Carol. *In the Midst of Parenting: A Look at the Real Dramas and Dilemmas*. Port Washington, NY: Brooklyn Girl Books, 2000.

Small, Meredith F. *Our Babies, Ourselves: How Biology and Culture Shape the Way We Parent*. New York: Anchor Books, 1998.

Spock, Benjamin, and Michael B. Rothenberg. *Dr. Spock's Baby and Child Care*. New York: Pocket Books, 1992.

Stepp, Laura Sessions. *Our Last Best Shot: Guiding Our Children Through Early Adolescence*. New York: Riverhead, 2000.

Sullivan, Evelin. *The Concise Book of Lying*. New York: Farrar, Straus, and Giroux, 2001.

Thompson, Michael. *Speaking of Boys: Answers to the Most Asked Questions About Raising Sons*. New York: Living Planet, 2000.

Tofler, Ian, and Theresa Foy DiGeronimo. *Keeping Your Kids Out Front Without Kicking Them from Behind: How to Nurture High-Achieving Athletes, Scholars, and Performing Artists*. San Francisco: Jossey-Bass, 2000.

Trillin, Calvin. *Family Man*. New York: Farrar, Straus, and Giroux, 1998.

Viorst, Judith. *Necessary Losses: The Loves, Illusions, Dependencies and Impossible Expectations That All of Us Have to Give Up in Order to Grow*. New York: Fawcett Gold Medal, 1986.

Wheelis, Allen. *How People Change*. New York: Harper, 1973.

White, Michael, and David Epston. *Narrative Means to Therapeutic Ends*. New York: Norton, 1990.

Wolf, Anthony J. *"Get Out of My Life, but First Could You Drive Me and Cheryl to the Mall?" A Parent's Guide to the New Teenager*. New York: Noonday, 1991.

Wooden, John, and Steve Jamison. *Wooden: A Lifetime of Observations and Reflections On and Off the Court*. Chicago: Contemporary Books, 1997.

INDEX

Photo © P. James Fotos

Michael Riera, Ph.D. (right), has worked in education since 1980. He is the parenting contributor for CBS's The Early Show Saturday, a national speaker on issues pertaining to adolescents and children, and has appeared on many national television shows including The Oprah Winfrey Show and The Today Show. He is the author or co-author of three books about teenagers, including *Field Guide to the American Teenager*. His website is http://www.mikeriera.com.

Joseph Di Prisco, Ph.D., is an educator and writer who has worked as a teacher and administrator for over twenty years in public, independent, and Catholic schools, teaching middle school, high school, and college students. The co-author of *Field Guide to the American Teenager*, he is also the author of two books of poems and two novels. His website is http://www.diprisco.com.

Both Riera and Di Prisco live in Berkeley, California.